# SHAKESPEARE-LAND

# Shakespeare-Land

*by*

W. JEROME HARRISON, F.G.S.

EDITED AND UPDATED
BY DR ALAN CROSBY

Warwickshire Books, 1995

© Warwickshire Books, 1995

Published in 1995 by Warwickshire Books, an imprint of Warwickshire County Council, Department of Libraries and Heritage, Barrack Street, Warwick CV34 4TH.

First published in 1904

ISBN 1-871942-14-4

British Library Cataloguing-in-Publication data
A catalogue record for this book is available from the British Library.

Typeset and designed by Carnegie Publishing, 18 Maynard St, Preston
Printed and bound by Cambridge University Press

# Table of Contents

# Acknowledgements

MOST of the credit for this publication must go to William Jerome Harrison, for exploring the Warwickshire countryside with his camera and for wanting to share the experience. We are grateful to Dr Alan Crosby for researching Harrison's journeys and for writing the comments on the original text; also to Mark Booth of Warwickshire County Record Office for offering his detailed knowledge of the history of the area.

In deciding to print a new edition of *Shakespeare-Land*, we were influenced by the fact that so many of the photographs which William Jerome Harrison used in his book were fortunately still available and in good condition. These are in the care of Birmingham Central Library and we are most grateful to the author's family for placing them in the care of the library, and to Peter James, Photographic Development Officer, Birmingham City Council, for allowing us to make use of such a large number of precious negatives and prints.

To supply copies of photographs not in the Harrison Collection we turned first to the Warwickshire Photographic Survey, of which Harrison was a founder member, which is also in the care of the Birmingham City Library. The County Record Offices of Warwickshire, Worcestershire and Gloucestershire and the Shakespeare Birthplace Trust were most helpful in providing material. The result is that the vast majority of the photographs which illustrate this edition were taken by the author or a photographer which he knew personally.

Courtesy of Birmingham City Library: nos 1–15, 18–21, 23–29, 31–36, 38–62, 64–69 and 74–80. Courtesy of Warwickshire County Record Office: nos 16, 22, 30, 37, 63,

70, 71 and 73. Courtesy of Hereford and Worcester Record Office: nos 72, 79 and 81. Courtesy of the Shakespeare Birthplace Trust: no. 17.

Patricia J. Dunlop
Warwickshire Books

# Preface

During the summers of 1881 to 1908, the pioneer photographer, William Jerome Harrison, strapped his box camera to his bicycle, took the Great Western Railway or even walked from his home in Coventry to explore the Warwickshire countryside. Pursuing simultaneously his interests in social history, geology, architecture, English literature and the new technology of the camera, he spent many an enjoyable day retracing steps which Shakespeare must have trod. The result is an informed and refreshing illustrated guide to Shakespeare's home country which reflects Harrison's enquiring mind and his unassuming nature.

The article and his photographs were originally published in 1904 as part of *The Complete Works of Shakespeare* by Henry Irving, pp. 137–265, a Fourteen Volume edition of Shakespeare's plays.

Many of the sites which Harrison visited remain little altered today. His description of Holy Trinity Church, Stratford upon Avon, for example, is as valuable a guide as ever. Other buildings are now in much better repair, having been taken over by the Shakespeare Birthplace Trust. On the other hand, two World Wars and the growth in population and transport in particular have brought about many big changes. A tour of South Warwickshire guided by Harrison opens the modern visitor's eyes to the pre-motorised countryside of a hundred years ago, as well as to the villages of Shakespeare's day.

A century later, some of Harrison's descriptions need further explanation in the light of recent changes or subsequent research. Without losing the integrity of the original text, Warwickshire Books offers the comments of a modern historian, Alan Crosby, whose own interests mirror many of those of the Victorian photographer's. To retrace Harrison's steps is itself enjoyable; one could not explore Shakespeare-Land in more congenial company.

## CHAPTER I

# Introduction to Shakespeare-Land

"Though Shakespeare's dust beneath our footsteps lies,
His spirit breathes amid his native skies."—*John Sterling*, 1839.

AN IT BE a mere coincidence that the same English county should have produced the highest name in literature of either sex—Shakespeare, and "George Eliot"? Although environment is but one of the factors in the development of genius yet it is doubtless a powerful one; and to trace its influence adds increased zest to the pleasure with which we visit and study the localities in which those whom the world has learnt to admire and to revere were born and bred.

In the pages which follow we shall endeavour to give some account of the sweet Midland region in which our Shakespeare grew up to man's estate; and which he loved so well that he left the pomp of London and of the Court while still at the zenith of his fame, in order to spend as much as possible of the latter part of his life within its pleasant borders.

> In 1931 the county boundaries of Warwickshire, Gloucestershire and Worcestershire were altered, and thereafter Stratford was no longer on the edge of the county. Ten parishes in the area south-west of the town were added to Warwickshire. One can still cross the Avon at the same point as Harrison, but it is no longer the county boundary.

**Extent and position of the "Shakespeare Country".** —In connection with Shakespeare the county of Warwick has usually received the whole of the credit which is given to the district wherein a great man has been born. But the town of Stratford is situated in the extreme south-west corner of the county, and a walk of ten minutes from the poet's birthplace will bring anyone across the foot-bridge

1
LOWER-LIAS
LIMESTONE
QUARRY NEAR
BINTON.

over the Avon and into Gloucestershire. Portions of Worcestershire, too, are close at hand; and the title (given by the bard's contemporaries) of "Swan of Avon" would seem perhaps more suitable than that of "Warwickshire Lad", bestowed on him by Garrick at the Stratford festival of 1764.

2 (OPPOSITE)
HOLLIES IN
SUTTON PARK:
[A Relic of the
Forest of Arden]

That exquisite river—the Warwickshire Avon—is indeed the distinguishing feature of the district. Rising near Naseby, in Northamptonshire, it joins the Severn at Tewkesbury after a sinuous course from north-east to south-west of about 100 miles. We may distinguish Shakespeare-Land as occupying a central tract, of which the Avon, running diagonally from Rugby to Evesham for 36 miles, is the leading physical feature.

**The Woodland or "Arden".** —On the north-west side of the Avon is the wooded region formerly known as the "Woodland", or "Wooland", which formed part of the famous Forest of Arden. In Saxon and Norman times trees covered the whole region from the Severn to the Trent; but

The division of the county into the Arden and Feldon areas, long recognised and highlighted here by Harrison, is known to be of very ancient origin. The Arden, the woodland region, had a distinctive and venerable landscape of irregular fields, winding lanes, scattered settlement and an unplanned, 'organic' quality.

great inroads were made upon the timber, first in connection with the salt industry of Worcestershire, and afterwards for use in the Staffordshire mines and iron-works. Large clearances were effected which offered desirable building-sites for the forest-dwellers, and in this Arden region Shakespeare would doubtless often visit the city of Coventry, with such towns and villages as Alcester, Henley-in-Arden, Hampton-in-Arden, Knowle, Rowington, Meriden, Wootton Wawen, etc., occupying the open spaces in a tract of woodland lying parallel to the Avon and about 15 miles in width.

Although it is possible that some timber was cleared to provide fuel for industry, recent research and analysis tends to the view that most clearance was undertaken to provide agricultural land and sites for settlement. It is clear from the Arden landscape that substantial areas of woodland remained until the nineteenth century. The main fuel for industry was in fact charcoal—which is more suitable for processes such as metal-working—and this was usually provided by the careful and deliberate long-term management of woodland to provide regularly renewable coppiced timber.

**The Cultivated Fields, or "Feldon", or Field Land.** —On the south-east side of the River Avon we find a fertile "champain" of field country, known to Camden and his predecessors as the "Feldon", a region of orchards and grass-lands, with corn-fields, about 10 miles in width, and containing such towns and villages as Leamington, Offchurch, Southam, Chesterton, Kineton, Brailes, Marston, Pebworth, etc.

The Feldon area derives its name from the Old English feld, which does not mean 'field' in the modern sense, but rather implies a large open area without hedges—an unenclosed landscape. By the sixteenth century it was becoming less open: the antiquarian John Leland, writing in the 1530s, reported that the area was 'much enclosyd, plentifull of gres [grass] but no great plenty of corne'. By the late seventeenth century, though, Feldon was described as 'somewhat barren of wood but very plentifull of corne'. In the eighteenth century it was a classic area for the parliamentary enclosure of open fields, producing the present regular planned landscape which still contrasts so markedly with the Arden district of Warwickshire.

Lastly, standing upon the very banks of the Avon, we have Rugby, Stoneleigh, Guy's Cliffe, Warwick, Charlecote, Stratford, Luddington, Bidford, Offenham, and Evesham.

Thus our youthful poet's "kingdom", with every corner of which he doubtless made himself familiar in the roaming days of his boyhood, occupies an area of about 36 miles by 25 miles, including some 900 square miles.

**Geology and Botany** —A glance at a geological map shows that the Avon roughly divides the red marls and sandstones of the Triassic Formation on the north-west (the "Arden" area) from the clays and limestones of the Lias to the south-east ("Feldon" district). The limestones of the Lias are largely worked at Wilmcote, Harbury, and round Rugby, and the thin-bedded stone has been frequently used in the construction of local churches, houses, and walls.

Harrison was particularly interested in geology, and was a leading member of several local and national geological societies. His superb collection of photographs includes many which relate to geological sites and features, and he regularly visited the quarries of Warwickshire to investigate new finds and record them photographically. The illustration of bedded lias in the quarry at Binton is typical of this aspect of his work.

All these rocks are more or less soft and easily weathered, and thus the country is of low relief, having swelling outlines and low elevations which hardly deserve the name of hills, Stratford-on-Avon is but 110 feet above sea-level.

The plants of Shakespeare-Land have been most carefully enumerated by Mr. J. E. Bagnall in his Flora of Warwickshire. The county contains altogether 852 species of wild flowering-plants, or more than one half of the total number (1,425) known in Great Britain. The plants peculiar to bogs and heaths are conspicuous by their absence; but generally speaking the county is still well wooded. In Sutton Park, north of Birmingham, we have a tract of land which has

3
THE AVON AT
LUDDINGTON.

never known cultivation, and here such rarities as the Grass of Parnassus, the Black Crowberry, the Cranberry, and the Whortleberry still linger.

In fact, Bagnall identified 1,309 species in the Warwickshire of 1891. Since the publication of Bagnall's lists the number of species identified in the historic county has risen to around 1,600. Many newcomers have arrived, some wild plants have been newly named, but because of habitat loss others have become extinct during the twentieth century. An excellent and very readable survey of the natural history of Warwickshire is provided by A. Tasker in his 1990 book *The Nature of Warwickshire*.

Among the rivers the soft-flowing Avon easily takes the first place for the richness of its vegetation. In summer its surface is here and there completely covered with the small white flowers of the Water Crowfoot: forests of bulrushes crowd its banks: and the Yellow Water-Lily, the Bitter-Cress, and the Water Meadow-Grass grow profusely. The grand oaks of Stoneleigh Park, and the hollies which flourish so wonderfully on the barren pebble-beds of Sutton Park (figure 2) live in

Sutton Park was probably a deer park until 1450. According to Tasker, it was 'a unique assemblage of natural habitats: woodland, grassland, pools and heathland...it is a jewel in Birmingham's natural treasury, and a reminder to the rest of Warwickshire of what was, until only a short time ago, a widespread habitat, taken for granted'. The loss of so much of the landscape heritage of parts of the county, as a result of industrial, urban and transport development, makes the survival of Sutton Park even more exceptional and valuable.

one's memory; but fine elms, chestnuts, and limes are to be seen almost everywhere. The south and south-east of Warwickshire is, however, distinctly richer in vegetation than the north and north-west.

Harrison was particularly attracted by the river Avon itself, and by the gentle rural beauty of its valley. However, when he was writing, in 1906, some of the rivers of Warwickshire were already polluted, especially those in the vicinity of Birmingham and Coventry. During the twentieth century the problem grew worse. Now remedial action is in progress, and the future is brighter. However, there has been much loss of habitat because many rivers and streams have been straightened and 'tidied-up', and are subject to rigorous management and flood prevention procedures, and in the long term this remains a serious threat to their wildlife.

The courses of the rivers are marked out by the rows of willows which grow along their banks (fig 3); and the acuteness with which our Shakespeare must have noted the natural phenomena of his country-side is shown by a reference in *Hamlet* (act iv, sc. 7):

Willows remain a distinctive feature of Warwickshire riversides, and many are still pollarded. Their crowns are from time to time cut back and allowed to regrow, to prevent them becoming too large and unstable: willows are notorious for their tendency to split and crack, and over-large branches can easily fall.

"There is a willow grows aslant a brook,
  That shows his hoar leaves in the glassy stream".

To a casual observer the leaves of the willow seem to be of an ordinary green colour, but a careful examination shows that the under sides of the leaves are whitish, and it is, of course, this lower side which we see reflected in the water.

4
THE RYKNIELD
STREET NEAR
STUDLEY.

The Roman road network of the county was somewhat more complex than
Harrison implies. Watling Street, the line of which is followed by the present
A5, was the main route from London to the North West. The county
boundary still follows the road for many miles on either side of Hinckley.
Intersecting it at right angles at High Cross is the Fosse Way, from Lincoln to
Bath and Exeter. It runs, straight as an arrow, across the heart of the county.
The so-called Ryknield Street (none of the names is actually Roman—all were
given by the Saxons) was part of the route from Cirencester northwards to the
Lichfield area. A fourth route ran eastwards from the spa and salt springs at
Droitwich, through Alcester and then on the line of the present A46 to
Stratford upon Avon.

**The Three Roman Roads of Warwickshire.** —The Roman roads of Shakespeare-Land are three in number. They
form a triangle, practically enclosing Warwickshire on the
north-east, the west, and the south-east. The famous Watling
Street, running from London to Chester, forms much of the
county boundary on the north-east side, from near Rugby by
Atherstone to Wilnecote. The Fosse-Way runs across the
Feldon, at a distance of about 4 miles east of and parallel to
the Avon, entering the county near Shipston-on-Stour, and
intersecting the Watling Street at High Cross (Venonis). The
third or north-western boundary road is best named the

"Ryknield Street" (figure 4), to distinguish it from the "Icknield Street" of the South of England. Entering Warwickshire at Bidford, it passes northwards through Alcester and the west side of Birmingham (where a portion of it is still called the "Icknield" Street): it is also perfectly visible, its course as clear as the day it was made (except, of course, that it is grass-grown), on the western side of Sutton Park, near the Royal Oak Inn.

CHAPTER II

# The Homes of
# Shakespeare's Ancestors

## I. THE SHAKESPEARES

"Shakespeare, a wool-comber, poacher, or whatever else at Stratford in
Warwickshire, who happened to write books! The finest human figure, as I
apprehend, that nature has hitherto seen fit to make of our widely diffused
Teutonic clay. Saxon, Norman, Celt, or Sarmat, I find no human soul so
beautiful, these fifteen hundred known years;—our supreme modern European
man."—*Thomas Carlyle*, 1839.

hakespeare's parents appear each of them to have
descended from a long line of local or Warwickshire "antecessors". Great difficulty is experienced
in tracing the genealogy of any but the very highest in the land before the sixteenth century. Parish registers—
upon which we mainly rely for the records of births, deaths,
and marriages—were first instituted by the direction of Henry
VIII's minister, Thomas Cromwell, in
1538, and were not generally adopted until
some twenty or thirty years later.

> Much detailed and important
> research into Shakespeare's
> family history has been
> undertaken by David
> Honeyman, whose book *Closer
> to Shakespeare* (1990) is
> invaluable in this respect.

### Ancestors on the "Spear" side.

—The researches of G. R. French, of Mrs
Stopes, and others, have traced "Shakespeares" in England as far back as 1260;
though the name does not appear in Warwickshire until 1359.
The origin of this surname is obvious, and it may well be that
it was bestowed on some hardy man-at-arms for his skill in
the management of his spear during the border warfare which
was so incessantly waged on the Scottish frontier in the

Middle Ages. At all events we find one "Henry Shakespere" dwelling near Penrith in 1349, and Allan and William Shakespeare in 1398, while the will of John Shakespeare of Doncaster (Yorkshire), dated 1458, which is preserved among the York Records, may mark a connecting-link with the Midlands. The first Warwickshire record of the name is rather unfortunate, as it is that of "Thomas Shakespeare, felon", of Coventry, for whose goods the bailiffs of that city had to account in 1359. The family must have spread rapidly in the county, for in the first half of the sixteenth century the name occurs in at least sixteen Warwickshire towns and villages, and especially at Knowle, at Rowington, and at Warwick.

This is a flight of fancy on Harrison's part. There is no evidence to connect the Warwickshire Shakespeares with those of the same name in Cumbria or Yorkshire, and the link with Doncaster is implausible—perhaps the fact that Harrison was born near Doncaster may explain his anxiety to establish that particular association?

11

**The Guild of Knowle.** —The "Guilds" which were so popular in England from the thirteenth to the sixteenth centuries, were societies or combinations which included all classes, and which had for their objects the protection and advancement of the interest of their members both in this world and hereafter. They partook of the nature of our friendly, sick, and burial societies; prayers for the dead were a great feature; frequent "feasts" were arranged—the origin of our modern public dinners; and during their latter years (they were suppressed, and their property confiscated, by Henry VIII at the time of the dissolution of the monasteries) many of them had assumed some of the duties which we now associate with a town council or corporation.

Honeyman points out that an Adam Shakespeare held land at Temple Balsall in 1359, and that he could conceivably—though this cannot be proved—have been a distant forebear of the great William. He makes a convincing case for tracing the descent of the playwright back to the Temple Balsall district.

Many guilds also had a very important role as trading organisations, seeking by restrictive practices to monopolise local crafts and businesses for their members.

6
THE SWAN
INN, KNOWLE.

Among all the guilds one of the most powerful was that of St Anne, at Knowle, a village 14 miles due north of Stratford-on-Avon (Knowle station on the Great Western Railway, 10 miles south-east of Birmingham). This guild in the year 1500 had 3,000 members, including the first people of the county, and with nine entries of the name "Shakespeare". Its register, on vellum, is now in the Birmingham Reference Library, and it has been admirably edited by Mr. W. B. Bickley.

The Guild of St Anne at Knowle was founded in 1412 by Walter Cook (born c. 1360), a local man who enjoyed high ecclesiastical office but retained his interest in and concern for local affairs. In 1396 he secured a faculty for the building of a chapel at Knowle, which had hitherto depended upon the church at Hampton in Arden, and this was consecrated in 1402. He and six other men jointly established the Guild and enlarged the new chapel—to be the parish church—to accommodate it. In 1416 he also founded a college there. The Guild Register for 1412–1450 has not survived, but that for 1451–1536 still exists, and it includes some 15,000 names. The Guild and College were dissolved in 1549.

The Guild-House or Hall still stands (figure 5) opposite the west end of the church of Knowle. It is a half-timbered fifteenth-century building, now converted into a shop and dwelling-house. The church of Knowle is a good specimen of Perpendicular architecture, embattled, with tower at the west end. It possesses a fine rood-screen.

In 1550, when the Guild no longer existed, the Guild House was sold and divided into private houses. By 1873 it had become a shop and served as the village post office, and in 1912 it was bought for the public, carefully restored, and was then used as the church meeting rooms. It is indeed a remarkable survivor from the medieval past of what is now a sizeable and thriving commuter village.

The Swan Inn at Knowle (figure 6) has good iron-work in its sign, and is a type of the old-fashioned hostels which are so rapidly disappearing before modern rebuilding and "improvements".

> Harrison's words here have an ironic ring. In the years after he wrote this the Swan Inn, or White Swan, a building of exceptional architectural and historical interest dating from the late fifteenth century, gradually fell into disrepair. By the late 1930s it had become derelict, and it was pulled down after the Second World War. Only the magnificent iron inn-sign survives, now gracing the nearby seventeenth-century Red Lion.

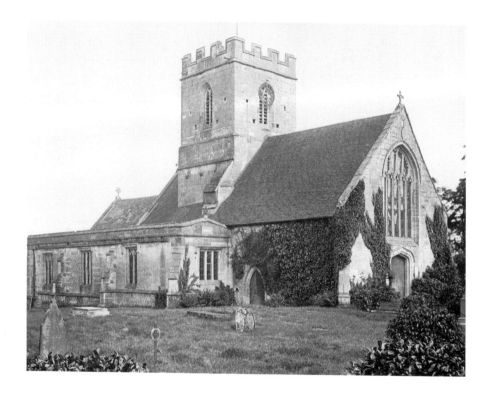

**The Village and Hall of Rowington.** —The pleasant village of Rowington lies on the east side of the Great Western Railway, just half-way between Lapworth and Hatton stations (2 miles to either). Its church (figure 7), dedicated to St Lawrence, has a central embattled tower, with a nave that is

7
ROWINGTON CHURCH FROM THE NORTH-WEST.

Rowington remains surprisingly rural despite the proximity of the new M40. The chapel seen in the photograph was added in the mid-sixteenth century, not along the nave or aisle, as would have been usual, but tacked on to the crossing and chancel in a quite different architectural style.

8
FONT, ST.
LAWRENCE'S
CHURCH,
ROWINGTON.

remarkable in that it is continued to the east of the tower. The present very uncommon plan of the building appears to be the result of a fourteenth-century enlargement of the original small Norman edifice. The early registers of Rowington are lost, but there are sixty-two entries of "Shakespeares" from 1616 to 1697, and the Guild Register of Knowle mentions "Thomas Chacsper" and "Johannis Shakespeyre" of Rowington in 1476.

On Rowington Green stands "Shakespeare Hall", a gabled, half-timbered house, said to have been the residence of Thomas Shakespeare, one of the poet's uncles, and it is locally believed that *As You Like It* was written in the little room over the porch. Certain it is that at the time of his death William Shakespeare was possessed of a copy-hold belonging to the manor of Rowington, but we know that he only acquired it in 1602.

Shakespeare did not own property in Rowington, as Harrison implies. His younger brother Gilbert, who died in 1602, owned a copyhold (a form of lease) on a tenement in Chapel Lane, Stratford upon Avon, which belonged to the manor of Rowington—in other words, the property, the lease of which Gilbert bequeathed to William, was in Stratford town. Shakespeare Hall at Rowington dates from the early sixteenth century, although it was extensively altered and extended subsequently. There is no evidence that Shakespeare had an uncle Thomas, but there is a strong possibility that the Thomas Shakespeare in question was the poet's cousin. Sad to say, the story that *As You Like It* was written there is likely to be one of the countless legends which have grown up around the name of the great man.

**Baddesley Clinton and the Church of the Expiation.**

—Baddesley Clinton, one of the most romantic, secluded, and beautiful spots in Shakespeare-Land, lies just a mile due east of Lapworth station (Great Western Railway). Its moated Hall is an exquisite example of a fortified manor-house of the fifteenth century. It contains much fine woodwork, and the heraldic devices in the windows are very noteworthy. The brick bridge by which the moat is now crossed was built in the reign of Queen Anne to replace an old drawbridge. The most is 8 or 9 feet deep, but underneath it there is a secret passage intended to afford a means of escape in time of seige. From the Saxon Badde the manor here passed to the Norman knight De Clinton. In Henry VI's reign it was acquired by one John Brome, a lawyer of Warwick, who, in 1468, received a mortal wound in a London church-porch from an adversary, one John Herthill, who suffered under a similar grievance to John Shakespeare's i.e. Brome refused to return a manor to its owner

9
THE CHURCH, BADDESLEY CLINTON.

Since 1980, the beautiful hall at Baddesley Clinton ihas been the property of the National Trust, which maintains the building and grounds to its customary high standard. As Harrison notes, the land was owned before the Conquest by a Saxon, Badde (the name means 'Badde's ley', or 'clearing'). The de Clintons acquired Baddesley manor following a marriage in circa 1225 and took their name in addition. In 1438 it was bought by John Brome, a Warwick lawyer who became Under Treasurer of England, whose fate is accurately described by Harrison, as is the subsequent violent history of the family. It is an outstanding example of a fortified and moated medieval manor house.

10
GRAVESTONES
IN THE
CHURCHYARD
AT ST
MICHAEL´S
CHURCH,
BADDESLEY
CLINTON.

under the receipt of its mortgage-money. In his will Brome writes "I do forgive my son Thomas, who, when he sawe me runne through in ye Whitefriers Church-porch, laughed and smiled att itt". Thomas dying without heirs, Nicholas Brome—John's second son—succeeded his father at Baddesley, and avenged him by lying in wait for and killing Herthill near Barford Bridge. This Nicholas seems to have been a man of violent passions, for a few years later he slew his own chaplain, "finding"—as Dugdale tells us—"the priest in the parlour

choking his wife under the chin". For this crime Brome had to do penance by rebuilding the towers of the churches of Packwood and of Baddesley Clinton. Nicholas Brome's daughter and heiress, Constantia, married Sir E. Ferrers in 1497, and then for twelve generations the Ferrers succeeded one another at Baddesley as heirs male, the last being Marmion Edward Ferrers, who died in 1884.

The Church of St James, at Baddesley (figure 9), is but a stone's-throw from the hall. It consists of a nave and chancel, with embattled western tower, mostly the work of Nicholas Brome between 1496 and 1508. There are some interesting old tombstones in the churchyard; and in Hay Wood—a bit of the old forest of Arden—east of the church, the Lily-of-the-Valley flowers profusely in the spring. But this is a strict botanical secret.

> Baddesley Clinton church was dedicated to St James until 1872, and then—at the time of renovation and restoration—it was re-dedicated to St Michael. An inscription records that Nicholas Brome "did new build the steeple in the reigne of King Henry the Seaventh". The adjacent woodland, which is indeed one of the few surviving fragments of the native woodland of Arden, is now known for its bluebells.

**Wroxall and its Abbey.** —From Baddesley Clinton it is just a mile walk eastwards to Wroxall. The abbey which stood here owed its foundation to a miracle! In the twelfth century Hugh de Hatton was taken prisoner while fighting in the Holy Land. On his promise to found a Benedictine priory for nuns, he was transported—fetters and all—by St Leonard in an instant to the woods near Wroxall. Unlike many people, he carried out his vow, and some relics of his priory—the refectory, the chapter-house, etc.—are still to be seen adjoining the present modern house, which was built by Mr. James Dugdale in 1864.

The house of the Benedictine nuns at Wroxall was founded in about 1135—the more sober historical accounts do not refer to the miracle! The fourteenth century ruins include those of what is said to be the chapter house, although Alexandra Wedgwood notes that 'no more than ten nuns could have been seated in it...perhaps it was the vestibule'. The nunnery was dissolved in 1536 and an Elizabethan manor house was built amidst the ruins. It was replaced by the present house, now a girls' school, which was still very new when Harrison was writing.

The Church of St Leonard is situated in front of the mansion. It is a stone building of the fourteenth century, with a seventeenth-century brick tower. It contains some good carved seats and stained glass. The village stocks still stand opposite to the entrance to the park.

The church was consecrated in 1315, and has good medieval stained glass. Parts of the tower date from the 1660s. Like many churches in the Midlands, it stands in the middle of a large park, immediately adjacent to a great house, and there is no village nearby.

The Knowle register gives Richard Schakespeire, and his wife Margaret, as living in Wroxall in 1464; and Mr Yeatman finds in the Court Rolls of Wroxall mention of an Elizabeth Shakspere as early as 1418. In 1504 the prayers of the Knowle Guild are asked "for the soul of Isabella Shakespeare, formerly prioress of Wroxall". The parish registers only begin at 1586.

**The Church and Hall of the Knights Templars at Temple Balsall.** —Temple Balsall lies between Knowle and Berkswell (2 miles from either). The Church of St Mary is an Early Decorated edifice of most beautiful and uncommon type (figure 11). In the reign of Henry III, Roger de Moubray gave the lordship of Balsall to the military-religious order of the Knights Templars, and they erected a structure to serve both as their hall and church. The interior is without either aisles

The church at Temple Balsall, with its very unusual history, has long been of note to antiquarians. It was very heavily restored—and partly rebuilt—by Sir George Gilbert Scott in 1849, but it is still a fine example of a preceptory of the Knights Templar.

19

11
THE CHURCH,
TEMPLE
BALSALL.

or galleries, and is one noble and lofty space, measuring 104 feet by 30 feet, and rising eastwards in four steps. There are large east and west windows; and a fine "wheel window", also, at the west end.

After the Templars were suppressed, in 1307, their estate here passed through several hands—including those of Katherine Parr and Dudley, Earl of Leicester. Finally it was given to found a hospital for poor women, which now stands east of the

> The adjacent hospital was founded in 1677 by the will of Lady Katherine Leveson, who died in 1674. The original hospital buildings were erected by William Hurlbutt, but were rebuilt in the early eighteenth century. The Master's House was built in 1836, the church in the 1840s by Sir George Gilbert Scott.

church. To the south-west of the church a barn includes part of what was once the refectory of the Templars. The little River Blythe runs close at hand, amid pastoral scenery which is very delightful.

### The Birthplace of Shakespeare's Father (Snitterfield).

—The village of Snitterfield is 4 miles north of Stratford, and 3 miles east of Bearley station (Great Western Railway). Arriving here some twenty years ago, equipped with camera and on Shakespearean study intent, we enquired of the old landlady

As usual, Harrison shows that he had a good eye for the details of church architecture. The fabric of Snitterfield church is mainly fourteenth century, the chancel (circa 1300) being probably the earliest major part of the building. Much of the church was heavily 'restored' in the late 1850s, the great period of over-zealous Victorian improvement work which in fact resulted in loss of, or damage to, much precious medieval architecture and ornamentation.

of the Bell Inn as to what notable things were to be seen. "Well, sir," the worthy dame replied, "there's our new billiard-room" —at which we fled!

As usual, it is best to make first for the church. The history of an English village usually centres in and gathers round its church. Its architecture, materials, additions, and restorations: the wood-work, iron-work, furniture, windows, church-chest, bells, and font; the parish registers; sometimes the subsidiary buildings attached to the sacred edifice itself; the churchyard—often containing remarkable trees and interesting tombstones; and the adjoining residence for the parson—all combine to reveal to the understanding eye an epitome of the history of the district, for, it may be, the preceding five or six centuries. And all honour to those who are in charge of these surpassingly interesting memorials of bygone England—to the clergy, with their humble helpers the parish-clerks, the sextons, and others. Not only do they feel a pride in, and love for, the sacred building itself, which leads them to guard it sedulously, but they are ever willing to act as guides to visitors, and to render them every possible aid and information.

Snitterfield, as the home of Shakespeare's father, John, and grandfather Richard, has a special significance for those who study the family of our greatest dramatist. Recent research by C. and R. Page, published in *Warwickshire History* vol. v (1982), has shown that one grandfather, Richard Shakespeare, rented his Snitterfield property from the other grandfather, Robert Arden. The site of the house has been identified as lying in the present Church Road alongside Bell Lane. The original house, in which John Shakespeare was born in about 1529, was demolished in the 1590s—during William's lifetime—and the present house was built on the site.

12
CHURCH
PORCH,
SNITTERFIELD.

Snitterfield Church has a Decorated nave, aisles, and chancel, with a Perpendicular tower and clere-story (figure 12). The fourteenth-century font is good, and there is much ancient carved wood-work. The double yew-tree and the three grand limes in the churchyard should be noticed; and also the three silver birches on the vicarage lawn, planted by the three daughters (and therefore now called the "Three Ladies") of the Rev. Richard Jago—a well-known poet,—who was vicar here from 1761 to 1781. Richard Shakespeare (the poet's grandfather) and Henry Shakespeare (his uncle) both farmed land here. The farm of "Ingon" and the enclosures called "Burman's Field" and "Red Hill" are associated with their names in ancient legal documents.

## CHAPTER III

# The Homes of Shakespeare's
# Ancestors (*Continued*)

## 2. THE ARDENS

"Then to the well-trod stage anon,
If Jonson's learned sock be on,
Or sweetest Shakespeare, fancy's child,
Warble his native woodnotes wild."
—*John Milton*, 1645.

hakespeare's Ancestry on the "Spindle" side.
—Shakespeare's father (John) married Mary
Arden in 1557. She was the youngest (and apparently the favourite) daughter of Robert Arden,
"husbandman", of Wilmcote, a village 3 miles north-west of
Stratford. This Robert Arden was the son of a Thomas Arden,
and one of the great questions in the ancestry of Shakespeare
is as to whether this Thomas was, or was not, the second son
of Walter Arden of Park Hall. Although, perhaps, it cannot
be proved in a way which would satisfy a court of justice, it
must be admitted that there is a fair probability of such being
the case. But the Ardens rank among the most ancient families in England, tracing their pedigree through sixteen generations from Walter Arden to Ailwin, the Saxon sheriff of

When Harrison was writing, Shakespeare's ancestry had been the subject of
comparatively little serious research. Since then David Honeyman and others
have painstakingly worked through the wealth of archival material now
available to try to establish his ancestral lines more accurately. Honeyman
considers that the identification of Thomas Arden (*c.*1462–*c.*1530) with the
second son of Walter Arden of Park Hall near Atherstone is 'effectively proven'.

13
THE ARDEN
COTTAGE,
WILMCOTE.

Warwickshire, and including great names and high connections. It must indeed have been a source of legitimate pleasure to William Shakespeare to hear—as he unquestionably would do even at his mother's knee—the story of the high achievements of his "antecessors".

The connection with the Ardens of Park Hall means that a member of the family rather less illustrious than those listed by Harrison may be brought into the reckoning—Shakespeare's presumed third cousin, Edward Arden of Park Hall, was executed for treason in 1583.

**Aston Church and the Ardens.** —Aston is now a northern suburb of Birmingham. The Church of St Peter and St Paul has a very good fifteenth-century tower and spire, but the rest of the edifice was rebuilt in 1891. The famous Arden Tomb stands on the north side of the chancel, next to the organ chamber. It has recumbent figures of a knight and his

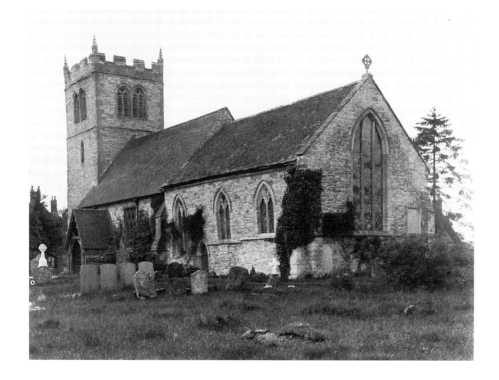

lady, the former in plate-armour of the time of Richard II—perhaps Sir T. Arden of Nechells. The Erdington Chapel, with the tombs of that ancient family, is on the opposite or south side of the chancel; and there is also a brass to Thomas Holte (died 1545).

14
ASTON
CANTLOW
CHURCH.

In Harrison's day Aston was a northern suburb of Birmingham: today it is an inner city area Fortunately the outstanding Jacobean mansion of Aston Hall has emerged unscathed from the upheavals around—once a country house well beyond the small market town of Birmingham, it is now isolated in a formal park amid the sprawl of the city. The famous Arden tomb in the church of St Peter and St Paul is a historical jigsaw puzzle. It has the effigies of a knight of the 1360s, and a lady of the 1490s, on a tomb chest of sixteenth-century date, and the seventeenth-century historian Dugdale commented that it was 'a faire monument of Arden removed from the priorye of Maxstoke'. It is therefore doubtful if the identification with Sir Thomas Arden of nearby Nechells can be trusted.

Aston Hall stands near the church. It was built of red brick by Sir Thomas Holte in 1618-1635, and is now used as a Free Public Museum for the city of Birmingham. Among the objects shown is a horologe which professes to be "Shakespeare's clock".

**Wilmcote and Mary Arden.** —The cottage, or rather substantial farmhouse, which is believed to have been the birthplace and early home of the mother of Shakespeare, stands but five minutes' walk from Wilmcote station (Great Western Railway). It is a two-storied half-timbered house with dormer-windows (figure 13); inside, the great wooden beams of the framework are worth seeing. But the most picturesque part is at the back, where an old dove-cot "composes" exceedingly well with a lofty cart-shelter and other farm buildings. The church of St Andrew is quite modern. The exact position of the land here known as "Asbies" which was left to Mary Arden by her father, cannot now be traced.

There is no contemporary sixteenth-century evidence that Mary Arden actually lived in the house which now bears her name—or even that her family owned it. That the Ardens did have property in Wilmcote is certain, and because of their considerable prosperity it is likely that they would have occupied a substantial house such as this, but the proof positive is lacking—the identification of this house with Mary Arden cannot be traced earlier than 1798, and there is some evidence to suggest that the family may have at one time lived at Snitterfield. However, the house (particularly since its restoration) is of major importance in its own right. It is a very large and impressive farmhouse of the early sixteenth century, with superb outbuildings, including the dovecot, with 657 nesting holes, which Harrison noted. It was a working farm until 1930, when it was bought by the Shakespeare Birthplace Trust.

**Aston Cantlow: where Shakespeare's Parents were Married.** —Wilmcote had no church in Mary Arden's days, and as the village is in the parish of Aston Cantlow, her marriage with John Shakespeare doubtless took place there.

27

> Mary Arden and John Shakespeare must have been married in about 1557. Although a number of Warwickshire churches are claimed to have been the place where ceremony took place, there is in fact no contemporary record because of the absence of early parish registers. The most likely location is thought to be Aston Cantlow, because this was the parish church for Wilmcote. In the church is the tomb of Shakespeare's aunt Katherine Arden, who married Thomas Edkins of Wilmcote.

Aston Cantlow is "Estone Cantilupe"—"Estone" because east of Alcester, and "Cantilupe" from the Norman family who owned the manor in the thirteenth century. Of many beautiful villages in this district, Aston Cantlow is remarkable for its "old world" appearance, and for its rustic and unspoilt cottages. Artists who know of this sequestered spot for the most part keep the knowledge to themselves—but it certainly is among the gems of "Shakespeare-Land".

> The story that John and Mary Shakespeare's wedding breakfast was held at the King's Head at Aston Cantlow does not appear in print until the late 1790s, more than 200 years after the supposed event. Unless some remarkable documentary evidence should turn up it must remain another of the picturesque but unsupported legends which have grown up since the late eighteenth century, when the name of Shakespeare first began to hold a special magic.

The grand old church of St. John the Baptist at Aston Cantlow (figure 14) is Early English in its architecture (late thirteenth century), and has some good fifteenth-century wood-work and a font. Close at hand stands the inn at which local tradition says John Shakespeare's party held the wedding breakfast; and exactly opposite is the very picturesque Court-Leet House.

## CHAPTER IV

# Shakespeare's Native Town
# of Stratford-upon-Avon

IN MEMORY OF OUR FAMOUS SHAKESPEARE

· · · ·

"Who wrote his lines with a sunbeam,
More durable than Time or Fate

· · · · · ·

"Where thy honoured bones do lie
(As Statius once to Maro's urn),
Thither every year will I
Slowly tread, and sadly mourn."

—*Samuel Sheppard*, 1651

**arly History of Stratford-upon-Avon.**—In the early times, when bridges were few or non-existent, the shallow places where rivers of any size could alone be safely crossed were sought out with care, and were usually marked by lines of stakes. The roads naturally made for these "fords", and villages and towns grew up around them.

A ford over the Avon at the spot where Stratford now stands was doubtless known and used in Celtic and in Saxon times. As to when the first bridges over the Avon here—poor wooden structures—were built, we have no record. There is a fair indication of a Roman cross-road running from Stratford to Alcester, and in later times the main or "mail" road from London through Oxford to Birmingham and beyond crossed—as it now crosses—the Avon at this point.

> The name 'Stratford' relates to the 'strata' or Roman road which crossed the Avon here. The road ran from Droitwich, via Alcester and Stratford, towards Alchester in Oxfordshire. The alignment of the road as it passes through the town is marked by Bridge Street and Wood Street.

29

The first record of Stratford-on-Avon occurs in Early Saxon times, when there is mention of a monastery here (probably on the site of the present church) belonging to the Bishops of Worcester. And from Domesday Book we know that a church existed at the time of the Norman Conquest. But of this monastery and early church no traces now remain.

The seventh-century monastery at Stratford seems to have disappeared entirely by the time of the Conquest. Neither is there any suggestion in the Domesday Survey of 1086 that a town existed at Stratford—instead, it seems to have been a small rural settlement south of the ford. There was a church, a water-mill, and a good deal of riverside meadow land. Then, as in later centuries, the hamlets of Shottery and Welcombe were included within Stratford.

**The Three Bridges at Stratford.** —The wooden footbridge south of the church has been rebuilt again and again upon the old foundations; while the adjoining Lucy's mill stands similarly on the spot where there was a mill long before the Conquest. Domesday Book writes it down:—"a mill yielding ten shillings per annum and a thousand eels" to the then Bishop of Worcester.

The wooden footbridge is now replaced by a modern successor, built in 1971 when Stratford New Lock was constructed as part of the restoration works on the Upper Avon Navigation.

The Clopton Bridge is a fine stone structure of fourteen arches (with five smaller arches under the causeway at the west end). It was built by a local man, Sir Hugh Clopton (Lord Mayor of London), in the reign of Henry VII, to replace what Leland describes, about 1540, as "a poor bridge of timber, and no causeway to come to it, whereby many poor folks refused to come to Stratford when the river was up, or, coming thither, stood in jeopardy of life".

A third bridge, of red brick, was built in 1826 a little below the Clopton Bridge to carry a since-disused tramway to Shipston-on-Stour.

Clopton Bridge has managed to survive the pounding it has received from twentieth century traffic in the years since Harrison wrote—although the town is now bypassed, and there is a relief road, the bridge still carries a great volume of cars and lorries. There were originally five more arches at the town end, making a total of nineteen—these were gradually filled in and turned into a causeway over the centuries. The little tower at the southern end is a tollhouse, built in 1814 when the road was serving as a major turnpike. Although much altered over the centuries this is a fine example of a major late-medieval bridge.

15
GRAMMAR
SCHOOL AND
GUILD
CHAPEL,
STRATFORD-ON-
AVON.

**The Guild Chapel.** —Almost equalling the parish church in point of age and of antiquarian interest, the Chapel of the Guild of the Holy Cross, the Blessed Virgin, and St. John the Baptist stands at the corner of Chapel Lane and Church Street (figure 15). The chancel dates back to the fourteenth century, but the rest of the building was rebuilt by Sir Hugh Clopton about the year 1500. In 1804 it was

16
FRESCO IN
GUILD CHAPEL.

found that the walls of the interior were covered with frescoes, including such subjects as the Day of Judgment, the Murder of Thomas à Becket, etc. These were carefully copied (and published by Mr. Thomas Fisher in 1836), and they were then whitewashed over again in the same year (figure 16). The north porch is an admirable example of late fifteenth-century architecture.

The Guild Chapel was originally part of the hospital of the Guild of the Holy Cross: license to have an oratory was granted in 1269. It was rebuilt in 1417–8, and then extensively altered, with the construction of the present nave and tower, in 1496–1500. Technically Harrison is incorrect in stating that the latter work was undertaken by Sir Hugh Clopton, because it was paid for, after his death, with money left in his will of 1496. In the chapel prayers were offered for the souls of deceased members of the Guild.

**The Guild Hall.** —Extending southwards from the Guild Chapel, along Church Street, is a long, low, and narrow half-timbered edifice, whose windows on one side look into Church Street and on the other into the Grammar School yard. This is the hall of the ancient Guild or Fraternity of the Holy Cross. A hall appears to have been built on this side in 1296 by Robert de Stratford, afterwards Lord Chancellor, and a great lover and benefactor of his native town; but the present structure is probably not older than the end of the fifteenth century.

The present Guild Hall was built in 1417–8. On the ground floor was meeting hall where Guild assemblies were held, while upstairs there were smaller rooms used for administrative purposes. Harrison notes the suppression of the Guild in 1547, and the legal transfer of its property to the community for civic and charitable uses. The upper floor became the grammar school (see below) while the lower hall was regularly used for civic events, and—from the 1560s onwards—for entertainments such as the visits of groups of players. The creation of the 'local body', referred to by Harrison, was known as 'incorporation'. After this time Stratford upon Avon was administered by the Corporation, or borough council.

The Guild of Stratford was not less important than that of Knowle (see page 12), and had become practically the governing body of the town of Stratford, so that its dissolution in 1547, by order of Edward VI, led to complete local confusion. As a result, a part of the property of the guild was restored in 1553, and a local body, consisting of a bailiff with fourteen aldermen, was established by royal charter to perform the work of a town council. This body met in the Guild Hall (figure 17) until the erection of the present Town-hall in 1768.

17
INTERIOR OF
GUILD HALL,
STRATFORD-ON-
AVON.

**The Grammar School of King Edward VI.** —One of the functions of the Stratford Guild was the education of the children of its members; and, to aid in this good work, Thomas Joliffe (a priest of the guild) gave some land in 1482, so that he is usually considered as the original "founder" of the present Grammar School. The endowment was confiscated when the guild was suppressed in 1547, but was restored by Edward VI in 1553. The school occupies rooms over and at the back of the Guild Hall (figure 15). It was open free to the children of all citizens of Stratford who were not less than seven years of age, and who were able to read. Without doubt it was here that William Shakespeare learned his "small Latin and less Greek"; and he probably spent seven years (1571–1577) at the school, leaving, it is believed, at the early age of fourteen in order to assist his father, whose affairs were beginning to be in an embarrassed state. The Old Latin Room (figure 18) stands over the Guild Hall, and has a fine timber roof with immense tie-beams. At its lower end a desk, traditionally

Although there is no contemporary documentary evidence to indicate that Shakespeare attended the grammar school at Stratford, there is little reason to doubt that this was in fact the case. William was the son of a prosperous glover, who was also a leading member of the Corporation, and socially and financially the school would have been the obvious choice for his education.

known as "Shakespeare's", used to stand; but it has been removed to the Birthplace. The masters of the school during Shakespeare's time were Walter Roche, B.A. (1570–1572), Thomas Hunt (1572–1577), and Thomas Jenkins, M.A. (1577–1578). The boys attended service in the adjoining Guild Chapel, and sometimes that building was also used as a school-room, which may have produced the well-known reference in *Twelfth Night* (act iii, sc. 2): "Cross-gartered? Most, villainously; like a pedant that keeps a school i' the church".

**The House in which William Shakespeare was Born.** —That the poet's father, John Shakespeare, lived in Henley Street in 1552 is proved by the corporation record of his being in that year fined twelve pence for having a dirt-heap of undue proportions in front of a house there. And that this house was the one standing on the north side of the street, and now known as the "Birthplace" (figure 19), may be taken as practically certain. In 1556 John Shakespeare purchased the adjoining house on the east side, and used it in his business as

a wool-shop; and in 1575 he purchased from one Edmund Hall, for £40, the Birthplace itself (previously he had only rented it). When the elder Shakespeare died, in 1601, the two Henley Street houses became the property of his famous son. From him they passed first to his elder daughter, Susannah, and then to his grand-daughter, Elizabeth, Lady Barnard (died 1669). Lady Barnard (the last of the direct line of Shakespeare's descendants) bequeathed this property to her cousin, Thomas Hart, and it remained in the Hart family until 1806, when it was sold to Thomas Court for £210 to clear a mortgage.

19 (OPPOSITE) SHAKESPEARE'S BIRTHPLACE, STRATFORD-UPON-AVON.

Finally, in 1847–1848, the property was purchased by national subscription for £3,000. In 1857 the whole was skilfully restored to as nearly as could be judged its original condition, assistance being derived from old illustrations and it is now vested—together with New Place and Anne Hathaway's Cottage—in a body of national trustees.

Shakespeare's birthplace, now perhaps the most visited and venerated literary shrine in England, was in a poor state of repair two hundred years ago. The reputation of the dramatist had been at a low ebb, and it was not until the 1760s, with the revival of interest in his plays and poetry, that the buildings and places associated with his life were seen as being of particular interest. The house was much visited by fashionable and literary figures during the early years of the nineteenth century, and in 1847—when there were some suggestions that it might be sold or even demolished—it was purchased as a national memorial after public subscription had been raised. As Harrison states, there is no absolutely definite evidence that Shakespeare was born in the house, but there is no good reason to doubt that this was in fact the case.

**Interior of the Birthplace.** —The early home of William Shakespeare underwent many alterations both inside and out during the time which has elapsed since its erection in the first half of the sixteenth century. The eastern part—the wool-shop,—as early as 1603 became an inn, under the title of the Maidenhead (later the "Swan and Maidenhead"); while for a time (1786–1792) the western house, or Birthplace proper, was turned into a butcher's shop.

At the present day some thirty thousand persons annually, gathered from almost every nation under the sun, pay willingly their nimble sixpences, and enter the ground-floor room, with its broken-stone floor, which a century ago was the "butcher's shop", and two centuries earlier still the "living-room" of the Shakespeare family (figure 20).

> The restoration of the 1850s was a remarkable exercise in its own right. The temptation to make too many 'improvements' was resisted, and the work was careful: the result is thus satisfactorily authentic. The main difference, however, is that in Shakespeare's time the house was part of a continuous frontage of houses and shops, stretching all along the street. The house is of timber and local Wilmcote stone, and was originally—as Harrison suggests—divided into a residential part and a workshop.

The kitchen, with its mantel-piece of solid oak, is at the back of the living-room. It has a cellar underneath, and two small rooms—the pantry and wash-house—behind. A narrow staircase leads from the kitchen up into the front bed-room—

20
THE
LIVING-ROOM,
SHAKESPEARE'S
BIRTHPLACE.

> The 'birth room' is now very different in appearance. Harrison's photograph shows it before the present furnishings and decoration were installed. The walls are no longer covered with thousands of pencilled names, although the signatures of Sir Walter Scott and other distinguished visitors are scratched in some of the leaded lights of the window.

the room in which the immortal poet was born (figure 21). Its walls and ceiling are covered with the pencilled names of thousands of visitors. The custodian of a century ago kept no "visitors' book", but invited one and all to leave their signatures where they would—and the names of Sir Walter Scott, of Washington Irving, and of others can still be seen. The custodian in question was a woman of vigorous mind, and on receiving notice to quit, she revenged herself by giving the room a "much-needed" coat of whitewash before vacating the premises! Fortunately she did not know or remember enough of the art to mix any size with her whitewash, so that it all dropped off again in a year or so!

21
THE ROOM IN WHICH SHAKESPEARE WAS BORN.

The bed-room behind the birth-room contains a portrait of no great value (probably an eighteenth-century copy of the bust in the church). The attics are not shown to visitors,

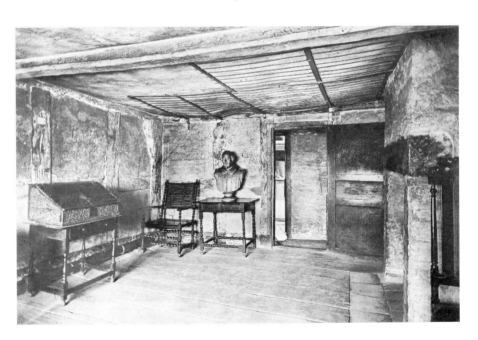

and some rooms on the west side of the house are reserved as store-rooms for the corporation records, and as a committee-room.

> In the past hundred years a great deal of further work has been done to conserve and restore the other parts of the house. Much of the fabric is unquestionably original, and the furnishings are fully in keeping with those which the poet and his family would have known. The wool shop is still used as the museum, and it still has the desk from the old Stratford Grammar School which Shakespeare is said to have used.

**The Museum (formerly the Wool-Shop).** —From the Birthplace we pass through a door leading from the living-room into the adjoining house, which was first John Shakespeare's shop and afterwards an inn. It now contains many interesting objects, such as a desk said to have been the one used by William Shakespeare while at the Grammar School: the "Ely House" portrait; many valuable deeds, letters, and other documents, including the only letter in existence ad-dressed to the poet—a request from his townsman, Richard Quyney, for the loan of £30, etc.

Shakespeare's house has been fortunate in its later custo-dians. We have a specially pleasant remembrance of the Misses Chattaway, and although their favourite remark when passing the copy of the poet's bust which stood in the living-room—"Plenty of room *there* for the mighty brain"—was made by one or other of them many hundreds of times yearly, it was always uttered with an earnestness and conviction which could not fail to impress the hearer.

The garden at the back of the house contains many trees and flowers which are mentioned in Shakespeare's works; and also the stone base of the old Market Cross. It extends to Guild Street, part of the main road from London and Oxford to Birmingham.

Because of the enormous increase in academic and popular interest in Shakespeare, his life, and his incomparable works, there was a pressing need for more facilities in the town for the study of the subject. In the late 1950s plans began to take shape, and in 1964, to commemorate the 400th anniversary of William's birth, the Shakespeare Centre was built adjacent to the birthplace. It houses the administrative headquarters of the Shakespeare Birthplace Trust. The Trust, an independent charity, is self-financing, and now owns several of the houses associated with the poet and his family. It also holds a priceless collection of Shakespeare material and local historical records. and the Centre includes the archive storage and reading rooms, a major library, and lecture theatres.

**A Peep at John Shakespeare: the Plume MSS.** —Of the "wool-shop" and of John Shakespeare a pleasant gleam of light has recently come to us across the centuries. Dr. A. Clark has discovered in the MSS. of Archdeacon Plume (born 1630, died 1704), now preserved at Maldon in Essex, an anecdote which Plume states he had in or about the year 1660 from Admiral Sir John Menns (1599, died 1671). "He [Will Shakespeare] was a glover's son. Sir John Mennes saw once his old father in his shop—a merry-cheekt old man, that said: 'Will was a good honest fellow, but he darest have crakt a jesst with him att any time'."

**New Place—Shakespeare's Home.** —We know neither the precise time of nor the exact reasons which led to Shakespeare's migration from Stratford-upon-Avon to London. We may conjecture that 1586 was the most probable year; and as for reasons, the depression of his father's business, and his own quarrel with Sir Thomas Lucy over an invasion of the latter's real or supposed rights in Fulbroke deer-park (not to mention the births, early in the year 1585, of twin children, Hamnet and Susannah), seem quite sufficient to account for the departure of one who must already have had some consciousness of his own great powers and some desire to test them in a wider sphere than that afforded by a little country town numbering only some 1400 inhabitants.

22
THE SITE OF
NEW PLACE.

And the date of his first return to his native town is as uncertain as the year of his departure. Surely he would be present at the burial of his only son—"1596, August 11, Hamnet, filius William Shakspere",—and we seem to have an echo of this visit in the draft of a grant of arms to John Shakespeare which exists at the Herald's College, and is dated 20th October, 1596.

William Shakespeare's ambitions were always centred in Stratford-on-Avon. To found a family there—a family equipped with that mark of gentle descent, a coat of arms,— this was his great desire. To achieve this object nothing was more desirable than the possession of a good house—the best in the little town if possible,—and this desire was realized in 1597 by the purchase from one William Underhill of an edifice known as the Great House, which had been built by Sir Hugh Clopton in the reign of Henry VII, and which stood at the corner of Chapel Street and Chapel Lane, with a good garden and an orchard behind it. This house was out of repair, and the poet paid for it but £60, but he must have had to expend a large sum in making it habitable, and he then rechristened it "New Place" (figure 22). It was for the purchase of this house that Shakespeare is believed to have received a very handsome present (Rowe, writing in 1709, says £1,000) from his patron, the Earl of Southampton. The main front of New Place faced westward to Chapel Street. Here Shakespeare took up his abode permanently upon his retirement from the stage about 1611, and here he died on the 23rd April, 1616. New Place then came into the possession of Susanna Hall, who entertained Queen Henrietta Maria here for three days in July, 1643. After passing through various hands, and being partly rebuilt by another Sir Hugh Clopton in 1702, it was purchased by the Rev. Francis Gastrell in 1753, who did not at all appreciate the great traditions connected with his new abode. First he roused the wrath of the people of Stratford by cutting down a mulberry-tree which grew close to the back of the house (a tree supposed to have been planted by Shakespeare in 1609), on the plea that visitors bothered him by asking to see it; and finally he pulled the house down on another pretext in 1759, and left the town.

By the time that the Rev. Francis Gastrell pulled down New Place in 1759 it had already been drastically altered and partially rebuilt, so that the house as it then existed was only loosely comparable to that in which Shakespeare had lived. From 1827 to 1872 part of the site was used for a temporary Shakespeare theatre. The purchase of the land on which the house had stood was the beginning of improvements to the site, but nevertheless it was, in the early years of the twentieth century, still a rather dull and unremarkable corner. Since then, however, careful landscaping of the gardens has accomplished its transformation, so that today there are smooth velvety lawns, long formal hedges of box and yew, banks of herbs and flowers, and an exact replica of an Elizabethan knot garden. The gardens are approached from Nash's house, now Stratford's local history museum.

The site of New Place was acquired by public subscription in 1861. Excavations have since revealed the old foundations, and these, with the ivy-covered well (figure 23), are all that

23
OLD WELL AT
NEW PLACE.

now remain. The whole has been converted into a pleasant public garden, in the large division of which are two mulberry-trees, descendants of the one planted by Shakespeare. This garden is certainly one of the most restful spots in Stratford.

**The Falcon Inn.** —On the other side of Chapel Street, opposite to New Place, stands the Falcon Inn, traditionally associated with the "merry meeting" of Shakespeare with Michael Drayton and Ben Jonson, at which the poet is said to have "drank too hard and contracted a feavour" which resulted in his death. But it can be shown that the "Falcon" did not become a hostelry until about 1654, and the cause of the death of the owner of New Place is to be sought rather in the poisonous emanations which must have proceeded from the foul ditch that then ran down Chapel Lane, just beneath his windows.

## CHAPTER V

# "Shakespeare's Church":
# The Collegiate Church of Holy
# Trinity at Stratford-on-Avon

". . . Here the bard divine,
Whose sacred dust you high-arch'd aisles enclose,
Where the tall windows rise in stately rows
Above the embowering shade,
Here first, at Fancy's fairy-circled shrine,
Of daisies pied his infant offering made;
Here playful yet, in stripling years unripe,
Fram'd of thy reeds a shrill and artless pipe."
—*Thomas Warton*, 1777.

he Parish Church of Stratford. —This beautiful edifice stands on the south side of Stratford, well apart from the noise and bustle of the little town. A lovely avenue of lime-trees leads from the "Old Town" gate of the churchyard to the fine north porch, which constitutes the principal entrance to the church. This porch dates from about the year 1500, and its inner door still bears a much older "sanctuary knocker", which once offered a safe refuge to the criminal who could take hold of it before his pursuers seized him. The outside of the west wall of the

The beautiful parish church of Holy Trinity is little altered from Harrison's day—the churchyard is perhaps tidier and the stonework a little cleaner, but not much else has changed. The lime tree approach remains a delightful feature, the architectural splendour of the church is of course the same. Inside there has been some alteration: the font, for example, has been moved to the north aisle, and the parish registers are now housed at the Shakespeare Centre. For the rest of this chapter, Harrison's intimate knowledge of church architecture speaks for itself.

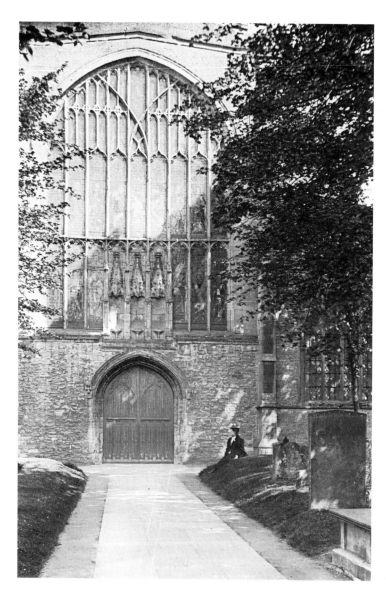

24
WEST DOOR,
CHURCH OF
THE HOLY
TRINITY,
STRATFORD-ON-
AVON.

porch bears several indentations, which are probably bullet marks, and record, it may be, the execution of some unfortunate prisoner during the Civil Wars.

**Exterior of Holy Trinity.** —It will be well to examine first the exterior of the church, and from the north porch

we walk along the north side of the building. The path is lined with early tombstones, some bearing the quaint heads of cherubs; but although we know that many of Shakespeare's kith and kin—his parents, his four sisters, and three of his brothers—lie here, yet there is no record of their places of interment. The old charnel-house, the thought of which so displeased the poet, projected from the east end

of the north wall of the chancel, but it was pulled down in the year 1801. Passing round the east end, we find another tombstone-lined walk leading round the south side of the church, and in the south wall of the chancel we note the priest's door. The path leads us to the west end, where the fine old oak doors are seen to be surmounted by a window of the same date (fifteenth century) as the north porch. This window is based on, and includes, three cano-pied niches, but the statues which these doubtless once contained have been destroyed (figure 24).

Returning to the east end of Holy Trinity, we find a walled river-side walk looking down upon the Avon, which flows placidly at our feet. This walk is lined by lofty elms, whose upper branches afford homes for a colony of rooks (figure 25). This is a peaceful spot; and, seated between the church and the river, thinking of the gentle spirit whose dust lies close at hand, and to whom this scene must have been specially

26
HOLY TRINITY,
THE NAVE,
LOOKING EAST.

familiar, we wonder what he would think of the fame which has accrued to his memory during the three centuries which have passed since he too watched the Avon glide by. To his reputation as an author Shakespeare seems, while living, to have attached little or no value, but on what a pinnacle has it placed him since his death!

**The Interior of Holy Trinity.** —Entering by the north porch, we at once note the cruciform arrangement of the edifice. The nave, with its lofty clerestory (figure 26); has north and south aisles, and at the eastern end of each aisle there is a chapel. That at the east end of the south aisle was dedicated to St. Thomas à Becket; but the corresponding chapel at the east end of the north aisle—the Clopton chapel—was, and is, much more important (figure 27), containing as it does the tombs of the principal local family—the Cloptons of Clopton

27
THE CLOPTON
CHAPEL.

House. The old font in which Shakespeare was baptized stands in the south aisle, and the parish registers containing the all-important entries referring to his baptism and burial are placed in the west end of the north aisle.

Leaving the nave and entering the central square which forms the base of the tower, we note the north and south transepts, and then pass through the fifteenth-century rood-screen into the chancel (figure 28). The old oak seats of the choir-stalls bear some curiously carved "misereres".

**The Shakespeare Graves.** —Advancing east-wards to the altar rails, we find beyond them a row of stone slabs upon the floor, which mark the graves of those who—with their families—had a legal right to be buried here, not by reason of any particular virtues which they might possess, but because they were the owners of the parish tithes—a position which was attained by Shakespeare in 1605, when he purchased a moiety of the tithes of Stratford, Old Stratford, Bishopton, and Welcombe for the sum of £440.

28
THE CHANCEL,
CHURCH OF
THE HOLY
TRINITY.

Next to the north wall of the chancel lies the poet's wife, Anne Hathaway, who died in 1623, at the age of sixty-seven; then comes her husband's stone, bearing the world-famous inscription:

> "Good frend for Jesus sake forbeare
> To digg the dust encloased heare;
> Blest be ye man yt. spares thes stones
> And curst be he yt. moves my bones."

The best proof of the merit of this composition lies in its efficacy. The writer's bones have lain undisturbed for three centuries, and although we are told that his wife and his daughter "did earnestly desire to be buried in the same grave" with him, yet the fear of the curse laid by the mighty mind had so prevailed that no sexton has ever dared to meddle with our Shakespeare's place of interment.

Next to Shakespeare lies Thomas Nash (died 1647), who married Elizabeth, the poet's granddaughter; and then follow the slabs of Dr John Hall (died 1635), and of his wife Susanna, Shakespeare's elder daughter, who died in 1649. The remainder of the space to the south wall of the chancel is occupied by the graves of two members of the Watts family, who were, like Shakespeare, lay proprietors of the tithes.

**Shakespeare's Monument.** —On the north wall of the chancel, almost directly above the place of his interment, stands Shakespeare's monument, consisting of a bust (figure 29) carved out of limestone by Gerard Johnson, the Dutch "tombe-maker" of Southwark. This bust is enclosed by columns of black marble, which support an entablature bearing the family arms, on each side of which a cherub is seated. An inscription is placed below. Dugdale's engraving of the monument (probably executed about 1636) in his great work, the *Antiquities of Warwickshire*, published in 1656, shows important discrepancies with its present state; but these are

29
SHAKESPEARE'S
MONUMENT,
CHURCH OF
THE HOLY
TRINITY.

probably due to the careless and incorrect drawing from which Dugdale's artist worked, similar errors as regards other monuments occurring in the same book. The bust has a somewhat unnatural appearance as seen from the floor of the chancel, and this may be its being a more or less literal copy of a plaster cast made after death. The fine photograph by

Chancel
ixt.

ha
the

Harold Baker, reproduced in figure 29, was made from a scaffold erected so as to be on a level with the face, and the features then present much greater refinement, and are not without a sign of humour, especially about the mouth.

### Other Tombs in the Chancel.

—Among other noteworthy objects in the chancel are the high tomb of Dean Thomas Balshall (died 1491), which stands against the north wall, and has above it a monument with two marble busts of Richard Combe and Judith Combe (his promised wife; she died in 1649); and the tomb, with effigy, of John Combe, upon whom tradition says that, being suspected of usury, Shakespeare composed the following lines (some years before Combe's death) as a sort of anticipatory epitaph:

> "Ten in a hundred lies here en-graved,
> 'T is a hundred to ten his soul is not saved:
> If any man ask, Who lies in this tomb?
> Ho! Ho! quoth the devil, 't is my John-a-Combe!"

### The Architecture of Holy Trinity. —Returning to the churchyard, and taking up our position at the best general point of view the north-east corner—we note the square central tower, eighty feet in height, from which the stone spire rises for another eighty-three feet (figure 31).

The entire length of Holy Trinity is one hundred and ninety-seven feet from east to west, and its extreme breadth is sixty-eight feet.

The transepts are the oldest part of the edifice, and may date back to the beginning of the thirteenth century.

Next in point of age we have the tower, the north and south aisles, and the nave piers: these were the work of the Stratfords, 1280 to 1330.

The chancel, the clerestory, the west window, and the north porch were built by Deans Balshall and Collingwood, 1480 to 1520.

The original steeple was of wood, and was only forty-two feet in height; it had become much decayed, and in 1765 was advantageously replaced by the present much loftier stone spire.

31
CHURCH OF
THE HOLY
TRINITY FROM
THE
NORTH-EAST.

## CHAPTER VI

# A walk through
# Stratford-upon-Avon

"Ye *Warwickshire* lads, and ye lasses,
  See what at our Jubilee passes;
Come revel away, rejoice and be glad;
For the lad of all lads was a *Warwickshire* lad,
      *Warwickshire* lad,
        All be glad;
For the lad of all lads was a *Warwickshire* lad."
—*David Garrick*, 1769

**rom the Station to the Fountain.** —Most of the visitors to Stratford-upon-Avon alight at the Great Western station, which lies on the west side of the town. Walking eastwards down Greenhill Street we soon see the clock-tower and fountain, the gift of Mr. G. W. Childs, of Philadelphia, at the Diamond Jubilee of Queen Victoria (1897). Of this structure—and still more of the Memorial Theatre, &c., and other modern structures in Stratford—it can only be said that they strike a very inharmonious note. One can but wish that it had been possible to reserve a certain tract, including all the old part of the town, within which no alterations or additions might be made without the consent of a national committee; a body which should also have power themselves to acquire property for desirable improvements.

> Opinions about the American fountain still vary but there can be no doubt that, however remarkable the structure might be, it is certainly not in keeping with the general architectural and aesthetic background of an English country market town. It was built in 1887 (not 1897 as Harrison states), and the first cupful of water was drunk at the unveiling ceremony by the great actor Henry Irving.

Among the old houses noted by Harrison and surviving today is Mason's Court, built in the 1480s and in recent years most impressively and faithfully restored to its original character and appearance.

The fountain stands in Rother Street—the old cattle market,—where John Shakespeare and his clever boy doubtless made many a deal in the skins which it was part of his business to convert into gloves, leggings, and such like. Two or three old houses here are well worthy of notice.

**From the Fountain to the Birthplace.** —Turning to the left we pass down either Windsor Street or Mere Street, and enter what is to many the most interesting street in England— Henley Street, on the north side of which stands the house in which, on 23 April, 1564, William Shakespeare was born. Notice that the house has been isolated (figure 19) by the removal of some modern cottages, while the pipes by which it is warmed come from the custodian's cottage, some little distance away—precautions which it is hoped may remove all risks from fire.

Harrison here refers to gas central heating and lighting. The risk of fire was greatly diminished once electricity had been installed.

**From the Birthplace to Bridge Street.** —Walking eastwards, along Henley Street, we pass Mr Carnegie's new free library (a building which harmonizes well with its surroundings), and find ourselves at the top of Bridge Street and in the

The free public library was a gift to the town by the millionaire Scots American philanthropist Andrew Carnegie. The building was in origin a medieval house, and by the 1890s was very badly dilapidated. In 1901 it was saved from demolition by the campaigning efforts of the immensely-popular romantic novelist Marie Corelli, who lived in Stratford. The interior was extensively renovated, and the exterior largely rebuilt, to accommodate the new library.

32
OLD INNS,
BRIDGE
STREET,
STRATFORD-ON-
AVON.

very centre of Stratford. Bridge Street leads down to "Bridge-
foot" and the Clopton Bridge, and on market days the stalls
placed in its wide expanse look quite picturesque. This street
owes its breadth to the removal of a "Middle Row" of houses,
some of which were standing as recently as 1858.

In or near Bridge Street are some famous inns—the "Red
Horse" where Washington Irving wrote, and where his "parlour", with its famous "sceptre-poker", is carefully preserved

In Harrison's day Bridge Street, on the line of the Roman road, was the main
centre for coaching traffic, and he notes several fine inns and hotels which are
also shown on the photograph. Since 1907 all the eighteenth century coaching
inns have gone, and the street has become the chief shopping area of the town.
The site of the Red Horse and Golden Lion is now occupied by Marks and
Spencer, with the impressive eighteenth century portico forming the store
entrance—even the portico is not original. When Harrison wrote his book it
graced the Shakespeare Hotel in Chapel Street, and was moved to Bridge
Street only in 1920.

in its original dignity; next door is the "Golden Lion"; the
"Old Red Lion" stands nearly opposite; and nearer to the
bridge are the "Red Lion" and the "Unicorn" (figure 32). The
truly "Georgian" building at the top of Bridge Street is the
Market House, built in 1820.

The Market House replaced the sixteenth century market cross (now in the garden of Shakespeare's birthplace), and commemorated the coronation of King George IV—the foundation stone was laid during the celebrations. It was always under-used, and in the late nineteenth century was considered to be ugly, inconvenient and outdated. It was threatened with demolition, but in 1908, in a very early and commendable example of the conversion of a historic building, it was taken over by a bank. One recent writer has described it as 'an object lesson in changing taste', since what seemed so unappealing to the Victorians appears to us to be a very attractive building.

## Along High Street and Chapel Street to New Place.

—Continuing our walk southwards we now enter High Street—the usual title for the most important street of any old English town.

At the corner of Bridge Street and High Street stands a much modernized house—once "The Cage", and the residence of Shakespeare's younger daughter Judith for many years after her marriage in 1616 with Thomas Quincey, who carried on here the trade of a vintner. The cellars are apparently unaltered, and the slope down which the barrels were rolled

33
CHAPEL STREET, STRATFORD-ON-AVON.

into them can still be seen. Behind them is a dark little room which may have been the actual "cage" or place of confinement for local offenders.

Although the house at 1 High Street was known as 'The Cage' there is considerable doubt as to whether it was ever the gaol—this is known to have been on the site of 5 High Street from at least 1330 until 1700, with a pillory and whipping post nearby. 1 High Street was called The Cage as early as 1470, and its cellars date from 1381 or earlier. The house was given extensive facelifts in the early nineteenth century and again in 1923. That it was the residence of Thomas and Judith Quiney is, however, a certainty.

**The Harvard House.** —Passing on down High Street we note on the right hand the exquisite, unrestored old front of the "Harvard House", with its carved wood-work, built by Alderman Thomas Rogers in 1596 (figure 34). His daughter Katharine married Robert Harvard, and their son John (born 1607) emigrated to America and founded the famous Harvard College there.

Fires in 1594 and 1595 destroyed many of the older properties in High Street, and Harvard House must have been rebuilt after these. Its rich carving has never been plastered over, and so represents the original appearance of a typical Stratford town house belonging to prosperous citizens of the last years of Elizabeth's reign. The original house also included the adjacent property, now Freeman Hardy & Willis.

**The Town Hall.** —Chapel Street (figure 33) is a continuation of High Street, and at their junction Ely Street comes in on the right and Sheep Street on the left. Leading out of the latter thoroughfare are some very picturesque old courts, which well deserve a visit, and which may be freely entered.

At the corner of Chapel Street and Sheep Street is a square stone building, which is the Town Hall. It was built in 1768— just about the time of Garrick's grand jubilee celebration—

and the great actor presented the statue of Shakespeare which stands over the entrance. In the Council Chamber upstairs are some good paintings, including a Romney.

---

The first town hall was built in the 1630s, and was badly damaged by the explosion of a barrel of gunpowder during the Civil War: it was demolished in 1767, when the present building was constructed. Originally there were open arches on the ground floor, but in 1863 these were infilled. It was Stratford's first significant Classical building, and was thus completely up-to-date and in very marked contrast to the half-timbered architecture which had previously been ubiquitous in the town. The Shakespeare Festival of 1769 marked the birth of the modern Shakespeare 'industry'.

---

**Old Houses in Chapel Street.** —On the east side of Chapel Street, beyond the Town Hall, we find several most interesting old houses, including the Shakespeare Hotel, the House of Five Gables (by many thought to be the best of its kind in Stratford—figure 35), and then those which in Shakespeare's days were inhabited by Thomas Hathaway, by Julius Shawe (one of the witnesses to Shakespeare's will), and by Thomas Nash (who married Elizabeth Hall—the poet's granddaughter). Nash's house had been purchased by the Birthplace Trust, and is now used as a museum, a small charge being made for admission. It contains an old "shovelboard", formerly in the Falcon Tavern opposite, and also various relics from New Place.

---

The Shakespeare Hotel originally had four gables, and was rather less than half of a very large and splendid sixteenth century house. It became an inn in 1766 and at that time was given a Georgian front, in the height of architectural fashion. In 1920 the front was removed to Bridge Street, and a mock-Tudor timbered front added in its place. The other part of the original building, the five gables to the right, was absorbed into the hotel in the 1880s. It is a fine and well-preserved example of the town architecture of the early sixteenth century.

---

34
THE HARVARD
HOUSE, HIGH
STREET,
STRATFORD-ON-
AVON.

**New Place itself**—the site of the good house in which William Shakespeare must have felt so much legitimate pride is surrounded by a handsome iron railing bearing the poet's arms, inside which we see the well by which the house was supplied with water, and a few wired-over trenches showing such of the foundations as could be discovered by excavating—and that is all. Not even a drawing, plan, or sketch exists of New Place as it was when Shakespeare inhabited it.

61

> The Church Street almshouses are probably the oldest domestic building in the town—only the parish church and parts of the Guild Chapel and Hall are older. The almshouses were built in 1427 by the Guild of the Holy Cross to accommodate some of its aged and infirm members.

**From Shakespeare's Home at New Place to the Footbridge.** —Church Street is the southward continuation of Chapel Street. On its eastern side, just beyond the Guild Hall, we see a row of alms-houses, a relic of the work of the famous old guild. On the opposite side of the street is Mason's croft, now the abode of Miss Marie Corelli.

> Mason's Croft was built in 1724 by Nathaniel Mason, a Stratford lawyer, and was extended in 1735 by his son. Marie Corelli, the celebrated and very colourful romantic novelist, moved there in 1901 and quickly became a favourite local character. She died in the house in 1924. It has since become the headquarters of the Shakespeare Institute, part of the University of Birmingham, and courses and conferences are held there. It is not open to the public.

At the end of Church Street we turn sharply to the left and enter Old Town. The picturesque gabled house on the left is Hall's Croft, once the residence of Shakespeare's son-in-law Dr. John Hall, a learned and popular physician. A few steps more and we pass the Town Room, and then Avon

> Old Town is, as its name suggests, the oldest part of Stratford. Here, close to the parish church, was the original village street. In 1196 the bishop of Worcester, John de Coutances, began to lay out a new town on the agricultural land to the north of the village, an estate which had been owned by the cathedral at Worcester since Saxon times. The new town was built according to a regular plan, with a grid pattern of streets intersecting at right angles, and with carefully-defined burgage plots of roughly equal size. This speculative new town, a commercial venture, was designed to maximise revenues by capturing trade passing along the old Roman road and making use of the ford on the Avon. It was a success: 'New' Stratford flourished and prospered, and has never looked back. But still Old Town, with its less regular and informal layout, serves to remind us of the distant origins of the community more than 900 years ago.

35
HOUSE OF FIVE
GABLES,
CHAPEL
STREET,
STRATFORD-ON-
AVON.

Croft—formerly the home of that able local historian, R. B. Wheler, whose *History and Antiquities of Stratford-upon-Avon* (1806) is still a most useful book.

In 1607 Susanna Shakespeare married John Hall. She and her husband lived at Hall's Croft, where their daughter Elizabeth was born in 1608. In 1616 the family moved to New Place, which had been bequeathed to them by Susanna's father, William. It is a very fine Tudor house which looks much as it must have done when Shakespeare and his daughter knew it. In 1949 it was acquired by the Shakespeare Birthplace Trust: the house and the delightful gardens are now open to the public throughout the year.

**The College.** —In the field opposite Avon Croft formerly stood "the College", a substantial stone mansion built in 1353 by Ralph de Stratford (Bishop of London) because of his "good affection to this town, being his birthplace". Here dwelt the monks who served in the adjoining church, which became

63

> The loss of the College, which must have been a building of very great historical and architectural interest, is particularly to be regretted. Although Stratford has retained a very large number of medieval and sixteenth century buildings, there has been some unfortunate destruction during the past 250 years. The medieval manor house of Stratford Old Town probably stood on or near this site. The house called 'Avoncroft' dates from the sixteenth century, although the exterior has been altered and its age is not initially apparent.

"collegiate", with a "dean", from 1423 to 1546. After the dissolution the building passed through several hands, and was ultimately pulled down, for no very apparent reason—for it was still in good repair,—in 1799.

### By the Foot-bridge to the Town Meadows and Bridge Street. —Circling round the west end of Holy Trinity, which we have described separately in Chapter V (see p. 45), we take our way down Mill Lane, past Lucy's Mill, and cross the Avon by the foot-bridge. The ugly railway bridge of the East and West Junction bestrides the stream a few yards lower down, and the station of this line is close at hand. From this point a foot-path, parallel to the Avon, and crossing the Town

> The East and West Junction Railway was one of the most eccentric and unprofitable railway byways of England. It eventually formed part of the Stratford upon Avon and Midland Junction Railway, which ran from a wayside junction at Broom near Alcester, through Stratford, to another wayside junction at Ravenstone between Bedford and Northampton. Its traffic—both freight and passenger—was always minimal, its profits non-existent, and its real value and purpose something of a mystery. In 1990 a relief road was built along the course of the old line and railway bridge.

Meadows or public recreation grounds, will lead us northwards back to the Clopton Bridge. This is indeed a delightful walk: the grey spire of Holy Trinity composes most beautifully with the profuse vegetation of the river-banks and little islands, to which the splashing of the water over the weir adds a pleasing note.

The remains of the Old Lock make an admirable foreground for a view of the church, and remind us of the time when barges came up the Avon from Gloucester and Tewkesbury as far as Stratford.

In 1959 the old locks at Stratford were filled in. The river was first made navigable from Tewkesbury to Stratford, with eleven locks, in 1636–1639. The waterway fell out of use in the 1860s, and the last commercial traffic was in 1875. Between 1950 and 1964, in a pioneering venture, the herculean labours of volunteers ensured that it was rebuilt and reopened for pleasure traffic as far as Evesham. Between 1964 and 1974 the navigation works were extended to Stratford, to link up with the Stratford-on-Avon Canal which had been reopened by volunteer efforts in 1964.

**The Shakespeare Memorial.** —The house with beautiful grounds situated north of and next to the church yard is Avon Bank, the residence of the Flower family, whose members have done much for Stratford and for the memory of Shakespeare.

Avon Bank was built in 1866 on the site of an earlier house by Charles E. Flower, a local brewer who was a great benefactor and patron of the Shakespeare movement in the town. In the 1920s the house and grounds were acquired by the Royal Shakespeare Theatre. They were later used for the theatre gardens, opened in 1975.

Next to Avon Bank the garish big building of variegated brick which was erected in 1879 as the Shakespeare Memorial—including a theatre, library, &c., strikes the eye somewhat discordantly; and this harsh note is echoed by the puffing of little steam launches which ply from the Bancroft (*i.e.* "bank-croft", or field by the river) Gardens adjoining. Within the Memorial Grounds is Lord Ronald Gower's fine bronze statue of Shakespeare (figure 36), showing the poet seated upon a pedestal, round the base of which are placed smaller statues of Falstaff, Lady Macbeth, Prince Hal, and Hamlet.

36
BRONZE
STATUE OF
SHAKESPEARE,
MEMORIAL
GARDENS.

This statue occupied the artist some twelve years in its execution, and was unveiled in 1888. The interior of the memorial (figure 37) is better than its exterior, and its collections of books, including very numerous editions of the plays, will, it is to be hoped, be steadily added to, so that students may find the place of real value.

In 1933 the statue of Shakespeare which Harrison describes has been moved to Bancroft Gardens, at the north end of the old tramway bridge. Nearby can be seen a short stretch of track, on which stands one of the original wagons of the horse tramway

37
THE PICTURE-
GALLERY,
SHAKESPEARE
MEMORIAL.

The first Shakespeare theatre in Stratford was built in 1827 at New Place. The tercentenary of William's birth in 1864 prompted calls for a more permanent and impressive theatre, and in the 1870s Charles Flower helped to finance a new building, much larger and more imposing than its predecessor. The new theatre was situated in extensive grounds alongside the river, and the winning entry in the design competition was the 'garish building' which Harrison notes, a huge Gothic pile with a high and asymmetrically placed tower. It was controversial from the start. The library and art gallery were added in 1881. In 1926 the 1879 building (but not the 1881 additions) was destroyed in a spectacular fire, and in 1930 a competition for a new design was won by Elizabeth Scott. It was, in a very different way, as controversial as its predecessor. Its great brick bulk, still oddly out of context in the setting of Stratford, and making few visual concessions, is still much criticised. The new Shakespeare Memorial Theatre was opened in 1932. In 1986 a further theatre, the Swan, was opened as part of the complex.

After passing the red brick tramway bridge, we soon arrive at the east end of the Clopton Bridge—here rowing-boats may be hired,—and from the Swan's Nest Hotel note the roads diverging east, to Shipston and Banbury, and north-wards, to Charlecote and Warwick.

Crossing the Clopton Bridge we find ourselves once more at our starting point in Bridge Street.

## CHAPTER VII

# Short walks around
# Stratford-upon-Avon

". . . This is the forest of Arden.
Ay, now am I in Arden; the more fool I;
When I was at home, I was in a better place."
—*As You Like It,* act ii, sc. 4.

 **o Shottery: The Home of Anne Hathaway.**—
The pleasant hamlet of Shottery lies about a mile west of Stratford. We may reach it from the Great Western station by turning to the right along the Alcester Road. But the nearer and pleasanter ways are by foot-paths, and first of which starts from near the station (just before reaching Albany Street), while the second leads out of Back Lane opposite to the end of Chestnut Walk. Nearing Shottery village we notice on the left hand the Manor House Farm, with a dove-cot in the garden behind. Under its great roof-trees is a large attic, formerly used, it is said, as an oratory, and here one author supposes the marriage of William Shakespeare with Anne Hathaway to have been first secretly solemnized in 1582, according to the rites of the then but lately proscribed Roman Catholic Church.

The thatched cottages of Shottery are both numerous and pretty, and there are many juvenile guides only too ready to

Before the First World War Shottery was a rural hamlet a mile outside Stratford. Since that time, as the town has grown, a tide of bricks and mortar has advanced towards, and almost engulfed, Shottery. Nevertheless the centre of the old village retains many of its rural qualities, and the footpaths which Harrison describes are still there—albeit much altered. There is no evidence at all to support the story of a secret Catholic marriage between Shakespeare and Anne Hathaway.

Anne Hathaway's Cottage is partly fifteenth-century, perhaps even older: there is clear evidence of the former great hall. Like many other buildings which are today called 'cottage' it was actually a substantial house, home of a prosperous family. As with other Shakespeare sites, there is no incontrovertible evidence for the claims made about it. In 1914 W.H. Hutton wrote that 'there is no doubt that the house belonged to the Hathaways, but whether those from whom Anne sprang cannot certainly be said. But the tradition is very strong, perhaps continuous, that it was here that the poet wooed his bride'.

conduct the visitor across a little stream to "Anne Hathaway's cottage" (figure 38). This building stands at right angles to the road, facing a pretty garden full of "Shakespeare's flowers". It has been divided into two, and even three, dwelling-places, but in the sixteenth century it was a substantial Elizabethan farmhouse, in which dwelt one Richard Hathaway, who, dying in 1581, left to his eldest daughter, Agnes (or Anne, for the two names were equivalents in those days), the sum of £6, 13s. 4d., "to be paid at the day of her marriage". The large stone chimney in the centre of the present building, which bears the inscription "R. H., 1697", was the addition of a later Hathaway. The house, indeed, remained in the possession of the Hathaway family until 1838, and has since

38
ANNE
HATHAWAY´S
COTTAGE,
SHOTTERY.

been occupied, as custodians, by their descendants, the Taylors and the Bakers. Mrs Baker (figure 39), who died in 1899 at the age of eighty-six, was known and esteemed by many thousands of lovers of Shakespearean traditions, to whom she had shown the quaint living-room and kitchen of the interior of the house (figure 40), with the bed-room above, which contains an old carved bedstead—"the bed on which Anne Hathaway

According to some sources Mrs Baker was a descendant of William and Anne Shakespeare. This cannot have been the case, since their direct line died out by 1670, but—as Harrison states here—she was almost certainly a collateral connection of Anne Hathaway herself, and her pride in the link was legendary.

39
MRS BAKER, A
DESCENDANT
OF THE
HATHAWAYS.

40
ANNE
HATHAWAY'S
COTTAGE: THE
LIVING-ROOM.

was born"—having a curious rush mattress, and hand-spun flaxen sheets adorned with exquisite needlework.

**To Luddington.** —This tiny village stands on the right bank of the Avon, about three miles south-west of Stratford. From the latter town we many reach Luddington either by the Evesham Road—turning off to the left as soon as we come to the point where Shottery brook crosses—or (more pleasantly) by a foot-path which starts from the East and West station. As to the latter, however, there has been some dispute about a "right of way", so that enquiry should be made before starting.

> The riverside footpath which begins at Stratford and follows the Avon to Luddington, and which was of uncertain status when Harrison wrote, is now a public right of way.

The present Church of All Saints (Decorated) dates only from 1872, but in its churchyard there stands the font (figure 41) of a much older church, in which local tradition had steadily maintained that the marriage of Shakespeare took place. The registers unfortunately, are lost, but the curate of this early church in 1582 was Thomas Hunt, whom the youthful bridegroom would know well as having been

41
THE OLD
FONT,
LUDDINGTON.

his master at the Stratford Grammar School. There are some beautiful stretches of the Avon just at the foot of the church-yard, and the old thatched cottages are exceptionally delight-ful in being perhaps a little more dilapidated than average! (figure 42).

Whether or not Shakespeare was married at Luddington must always remain the subject of debate, and the mystery will never be solved because of the absence of contemporary parish registers here and at other possible churches. Luddington would certainly be a strong candidate—although, as Harrison says, the present church was built in the 1870s and so cannot have been the building in question. The font from the old church is now housed in the present building, as it was deteriorating when kept outside.

**To Billesley Church and Hall.** —We can reach Billesley by a four mile walk north-west from Stratford, but it is only two miles from Wilmcote station. The funny-looking little church of brick, with stone quoins (figure 43), was built in 1692, upon the site of an older edifice in which it is claimed by some that Shakespeare was married. The grounds for this belief are not very obvious, but one is that

42
OLD COTTAGES
AT
LUDDINGTON.

Shakespeare's granddaughter Elizabeth (widow of Thomas Nash) certainly chose this place for her second marriage with John Barnard, 5th June 1649. Tradition also strangely connects Shakespeare's name with the adjoining Elizabethan mansion, known as Billesley Hall, once the residence of the Trussel family (connections of the poet), which contains a panelled room, some good carved chimney-pieces, and a "Priest's Hiding-hole".

When Billesley church was constructed in 1692 much material from the older building was re-used in the fabric, and there is a possibility that the apse of the present structure (visible on the right of the building in the photograph) echoes the form of a Norman or medieval predecessor. The hall, now a hotel, was almost completely rebuilt in 1616–20 by Sir Robert Lee, son of a London merchant. The Trussel family were the lords of the manor until this period, and the old name for the parish was Billesley Trussel.

### To Clopton House, Welcombe, and the Dingles.

—From Guild Street—the back of the Birthplace—turn to the right up the Clopton Road, and in less than a mile you will stand in front of Clopton House. Of the original manor house of the great Clopton family (built about 1490) only a

73

43
BILLESLEY
CHURCH FROM
THE
SOUTH-WEST.

porch at the back remains. The rest of the house was rebuilt by Sir Edward Walker about 1665, and again "restored" about 1830. Various traditions cling round this building. It may have suggested to the great dramatist the "lord's house" in the *Taming of the Shrew* (a play full of local allusions). In a spring at the back of the house one Margaret Clopton is said to have drowned herself in the sixteenth century—and the story is, of course, connected with that of love-lorn Ophelia. Certain it is that the house was rented, in 1605, by Ambrose Rookwood of Gunpowder Plot notoriety, and that when the bailiff of Stratford searched the place in that year, he found a host of "popish vestments", which were apparently intended for the celebration of mass in a room in the roof used as a chapel, and which still exists as an attic.

From Clopton House a foot-path takes us eastward round Clopton Tower, and then skirts a belt of trees leading to the Obelisk, a monument, one hundred and twenty feet high, erected in 1873 in memory of Mr Mark Philips and his brother, who built the big red-brick house (Welcombe House) seen just below. A foot-path leads southwards, back to Stratford, and on its eastern side we see the immense trench-like hollows, called "The Dingles", which may be in part natural, in part an Early British fortification.

Mark Philips was a cotton manufacturer from Manchester who in 1867 had bought the Welcombe estate as a country property. He built Welcombe House, now a hotel, at a cost of £35,000, but did not live long to enjoy life as a country gentleman. He died in 1873, and the memorial to him was in fact erected in 1876. The current view is that there are no ancient earthworks on the hill and that the Dingles are a natural phenomenon.

**To Clifford Chambers.** —Pleasantly placed on the west bank of the River Stour, and about two miles south of Stratford, Clifford Chambers is easily reached by going over either the Clopton Bridge or the tram bridge, passing along the Shipston road, and them taking the first turn on the right

Clifford Chambers is still an attractive village, saved from development because it is on a side lane which is not a through road. Although Harrison says that the rectory is of fourteenth century date, Alexandra Wedgwood considers that it is a sixteenth century hall-type timber-framed building. She also contradicts Harrison's view that the south doorway of the church is Saxon, noting that it is, with other work in the church, of Norman date.

after crossing the railway. It had a small and very ancient church, with a Saxon arch over the south door. In the chancel are the tombs and brasses of the Raynsford family, of whom Sir Henry Raynsford is remembered as the intimate friend of Michael Drayton, who was in the habit of spending part of every summer here. The black and white half-timbered house near the church is the old vicarage, of fourteenth century date. It is on record that a "John Shakespeare" dwelt in this house in 1564, and if this was the Stratford glover it is just possible that his son William was born here.

The possibility that Shakespeare was born here can be discounted—there is no evidence to support it apart from the presence of a John Shakespeare, and there is nothing to suggest that this was the Stratford glover of that name.

The return to Stratford may be made by a path leading to the foot-bridge below the church.

**To Weston and Welford.** —"Weston-upon-Avon" is situated on the southern bank of the river, three miles south-west of Stratford, and nearly opposite Luddington. It is best reached by way of the foot-bridge, afterwards going under the railway bridge, and so onwards by delightful field-paths and lanes. Or Milcote station (Great Western Railway) is less than a mile from Weston church. The church contains brasses of the Grevilles (1523–1559).

> Weston is no longer near a railway station, but it can still be reached by footpaths and bridle paths along the Avon from Stratford. The boundary changes of 1931 transferred Weston, and nearby Welford, to Warwickshire from Gloucestershire.

Welford village lies half a mile west of Weston, within a great bow of the Avon; both these villages are in Gloucestershire. Welford is much favoured by artists, and its thatched and beflowered cottages (figure 44), its mill, its church with an excellent old lych-gate, and its May-pole, unite to make the whole a scene of beauty. The church (restored) includes some good Norman work, and the parish register, under the date of July, 1588, contains a vivid account of a great flood of the Avon, a flood which it had been thought is referred to in *Midsummer Night's Dream*, act ii, sc. 1.

The return to Stratford may be made by crossing the Avon at Binton bridge (Binton station on East and West line is close at hand) and turning to the right. At the south end of the bridge note an inn with a curious sign, the "Four Alls" (king, parson, soldier, and farmer), and the inscription:

> "Rule all: Pray all:
> Fight all: Pay all".

> Welford is said by one recent writer to have "lost its rustic charm decades ago", and to resemble a film set. It has grown rapidly since the Second World War, as a dormitory for Stratford, and and this has brought many changes. Despite this its attractive position and many thatched and half-timbered cottages ensure that it is much admired, particularly since the re-opening of the upper Avon to navigation in the 1970s, bringing many waterborne visitors. The lych-gate is said to be the oldest in the country.

44
COTTAGES AT
WELFORD-ON-
AVON.

Binton village is half a mile north of the bridge. Its church (Early English) was rebuilt in 1875; it contains some old stone coffin lids of the thirteenth and fourteenth centuries.

**To Charlecote: the Home of the Lucys.** —The     noble Hall of Charlecote, with the adjoining church and village, stands on the south bank of the Avon, about four miles north-

The inn at Binton, with its unusual name, no longer has the sign which Harrison describes, and there is no longer a railway station either. Harrison included that information so that walkers who were rambling through Shakespeare land could consider catching the train back to Stratford, but since Binton, on the East and West Junction Railway, had only three trains a day it is questionable whether the service would have been of much real benefit.

77

east of Stratford. Crossing the Clopton bridge, we turn sharply to the left, and soon pass the bathing-place and the villages of Tiddington and Alveston. In the chancel of the (disused) old church at Alveston is the effigy of Nicholas Lane, who brought an action at law against John Shakespeare in 1587. Arriving at the Charlecote lodge gates, we may either enter the park there or (better) keep on the road for some distance farther, so as to approach the hall by its principal entrance. Here we find a very good gate house, built—like the hall—of red brick, with stone quoins. Behind it lies the formal garden, and then we see the hall (figure 45) in shape like the letter E (a compliment to Queen Elizabeth).

45
THE HALL, CHARLECOTE.

For many years there have been claims, or rumours, that in the Lane tomb at Alveston old church there might be documents relating to Shakespeare. The tantalising possibility of undiscovered plays, or perhaps of legal material relating to the poet's life, was put forward. Predictably, investigations a few years ago failed to reveal any trace.

46
CHARLECOTE:
THE GREAT
HALL.

The Lucy family has owned Charlecote since the manor was granted to Walter de Cherlecote in 1190, and the present hall was built or rebuilt by the first Sir Thomas Lucy (born 1532, died 1600) in 1558. In 1572 Elizabeth visited Charlecote while on her way to Compton Wyniates. The interior of the

The magnificent house at Charlecote has been in the care of the National Trust since 1945, when it was generously presented by Sir Montgomerie Fairfax-Lucie. Claims that houses shaped like a letter 'E' were so designed to honour Queen Elizabeth are common, but cannot usually be substantiated—there are sound architectural reasons for such a plan. The gatehouse, noted by Harrison, is the only feature from Shakespeare's time which survives intact. The remainder, including the house itself, was extensively altered from the 1820s onwards, to produce a remarkable example of 'Elizabethan Revival' architecture—it shows what was considered to be authentic by those of fashionable taste in the early nineteenth century. The work, which involved the refitting of every room, took more than fifteen years.

hall contains some fine rooms, including the Great Hall (figure 45), in which are many historical family portraits and other paintings by Vandyke, Lely, Kneller, &c. The dining room and the library were added in 1833.

The Lucy crest consists of three pikes, or "luces" as the fish is locally named. This crest is well displayed in the large bay window which lights the Great Hall, and is shown upon the family seal. The house contains other gems, including a suite of furniture in ebony and ivory presented by Elizabeth to the Earl of Dudley, and brought here from Kenilworth, and an inlaid table from the Borghese Palace at Rome, which is said to contain as a centre the largest known onyx.

The park surrounding Charlecote Hall includes about two hundred acres and contains splendid elms, a fine lime tree avenue, and many red deer.

The church (on the eastern margin of the park) is a Decorated edifice dating only from 1833, but a Saxon font stands in the porch under the belfry, and in a dark mortuary chapel on the north side of the chancel are the ancient tombs of the first Sir Thomas Lucy, "Shakespeare's persecutor" as he has been called; of his son (Sir Thomas, died 1605); and of his grandson (Sir Thomas, died 1640).

Half a mile west of Charlecote village a bridge spans the Avon, leading to the village of Hampton Lucy, which had a pretentious modern church (Decorated), rebuilt by Rickman in 1826, and restored by Scott in 1858. From this point the return to Stratford may be made by a most charming foot-path passing through the northern part of Charlecote Park, and leading to a ferry at Alveston. Or the walk may be extended a couple of miles northwards in the direction of Warwick as far as Fulbroke, where the

Harrison clearly had a low opinion of Hampton Lucy parish church. Architectural fashions alter, and opinions alter accordingly. By the late 1960s, Rickman was generally considered an architect of great distinction and significance, and Hampton Lucy church was described as his 'magnum opus'.

park was situated in which Shakespeare is supposed to have conducted his deer stealing expedition.

> There is no longer a ferry at Alveston, and to return to Stratford on foot involves both a longer detour and—whether on the right or left bank of the Avon—a walk for two miles along a busy main road. Times have indeed changed.

**"Shakespeare no Deerstealer."** —Much of the charm which clings to Charlecote is due to the traditional feud between the first Sir Thomas Lucy and the Shakespeare family. John Shakespeare seems to have adhered—more or less secretly, as all the Roman Catholics were forced to do in those days—to the faith in which he had been brought up, while the knight of Charlecote was a red-hot Protestant.

> The debate about whether or not John Shakespeare was secretly a Catholic continues. David Honeyman is very sceptical. This was not an area in which strong Catholic beliefs continued, and since John Shakespeare was an important member of Stratford Corporation his loyalty would have been unquestioned.

And John Shakespeare's eldest son, William, like most young men in the pride of their strength, was doubtless fond of a "bit of sport", and so came into contact with the game-preserving land-owner. The tradition of a deep quarrel between Sir Thomas Lucy and the young poet is a Stratford story which goes back into the sixteenth century, and the explanation probably lies in the fact, always stoutly insisted on by the local gossips, that young Shakespeare hunted and killed the deer *in Fulbroke Park*. This park lies on the opposite side of the Avon to Charlecote, and about a quarter of a mile higher up the river. At the time of which we write it was a kind of no-man's land, having belonged to one Sir Francis Englefield, a proscribed and attainted man; and although it afterwards passed to the Lucys, it was not as yet their property, and no one could be legally convicted of trespass therein. But land-owners have never stuck at trifles, and the influential knight of Charlecote doubtless felt highly indignant that the son of any Stratford shopkeeper should presume to interfere with his lordly sport. Thus, though Will Shakespeare did both chase and slay the deer in the ardent days of his youth, yet he was "no deerstealer", for there was no legal owner of the deer which he killed.

> Even if John Shakespeare was a Catholic, it is difficult to see how this would have had any implications for the alleged poaching by William—that was a serious offence on the part of the son irrespective of the faith of the father. The story is an ancient one—unlike most of the Shakespeare stories—and there is clear evidence that William knew a good deal about the Lucys, as the references in several plays indicate.

Still, a magnate of great local influence like Sir Thomas Lucy was doubtless able to "make things warm" for the youthful deer hunter, and even to drive him from the district—an act of persecution which Shakespeare repaid with interest later on by holding up Sir Thomas to ridicule as "Mr Justice Shallow", with the "luces", or pike, for his coat of arms, in the *Merry Wives of Windsor*, and again in *2 Henry IV*.

## CHAPTER VIII

# Warwick and its castle:
# with the Beauchamp Chapel
# and Guy's Cliffe

"What needs my Shakespeare for his honour'd bones,
The labour of an age in pilèd stones?
Or that his hallow'd relics should be hid
Under a star-ypointing pyramid?
Dear son of Memory, great heir of Fame,
What need'st thou such weak witness of thy name?
Thou, in our wonder and astonishment,
Hast built thyself a life-long monument.
                                        —*Milton*, 1630

**he Capital of Warwickshire.** —Occupying a fairly central position, Warwick is well situated as the "capital" of the county which is named after it. Lying on the west bank of the Avon, it is connected with what might be called its "residential suburb" of Leamington on the other side of the river by a tramway. The Great Western line had a station on the north side of Warwick itself, while the North-Western station, called "Milverton", lies half-way between Warwick and Leamington.

The Leamington and Warwick tramway was opened in 1881, linking High Street, Warwick, with Leamington railway station. It was originally horse-powered, but in 1905 was converted to electric traction. The line was short, and after the First World War it suffered severe competition from motor buses. The tramway closed in August 1930. It is described in detail in a booklet by S. Swingle and K. Turner (Oakwood Press, 1978).

Approaching Warwick by the Leamington road from the east, we note on the left hand the ivy-covered house and gates

83

47
THE EAST
GATE,
WARWICK.

of St. John's Hospital, dating from 1620. Soon we reach the
East Gate, next to which is the fine house in which Walter
Savage Landor was born in 1775 (figure 47).
Perched on the top of the East Gate is the
Chapel of St. Peter, badly restored in 1788.
Passing through East Gate, we enter Jury
Street, and the stillness of the old town
settles upon us. We have heard an irrever-
ent militiaman declare its thoroughfares to

The original St John's hospital
was founded in about 1175,
but the present building was
erected for the Stoughton
family in the mid-1620s and
now forms part of
Warwickshire Museum.

84

48
THE WEST
GATE AND
LEYCESTER
HOSPITAL,
WARWICK.

be "too quiet for a funeral!" High Street is a continuation of Jury Street, and is terminated by the West Gate, which is crowned by the Chapel of St. James (figure 48). Of the walls which formerly encircled the town of Warwick few traces now remain.

The lower part of the East Gate dates from the early fifteenth century but most of the building was, as Harrison states, rebuilt in the 1780s. This work gives another indication of the changes in architectural fashion. Harrison evidently disapproves of the late eighteenth century restoration and rebuilding, and particularly of the chapel, whereas Wedgwood singles out for special praise 'Francis Hiorn's delightful chapel of St Peter [which is] particularly fanciful'. The architectural writer and historian Alec Clifton-Taylor, who loved Warwick, thought that the chapel was 'rather amusing and most original'.

Adjoining the West Gate is the Leycester Hospital (figure 48), a half-timbered edifice once serving as the Hall of the

85

Guilds, but granted to Robert Dudley, Earl of Leicester, by the Corporation, and adapted by him to serve as an asylum for twelve poor brethren (old soldiers by choice) with a master. The front bears the letters "R. L.", and the date 1571. On Sundays the brethren wear their dark blue gowns and silver badges with Leicester's arms—the "bear and ragged staff".

The first West Gate was built before 1129, and at that date there was already a chapel over it. It was extensively altered and rebuilt at several times during the medieval period, and in consequence it is now a jigsaw puzzle of architectural periods. The tunnel vault, for example, has three different sections dating from different periods.

The interior of the Hospital is extremely interesting, and the objects shown include a carved Saxon chair, a black oak cabinet formerly in Kenilworth Castle, and (in the garden) a fine old Norman arch and an Egyptian vase from Warwick Castle.

Leycester's hospital is perhaps the most picturesque group of buildings in Warwick, and its irregular and varied half-timbered frontage appears on many a postcard. Robert Dudley, Earl of Leicester, the favourite of Queen Elizabeth I, took over the fourteenth-century buildings of the former guilds of the Holy Trinity, St George the Martyr, and the Virgin Mary, and extended and altered them to accommodate his new charitable foundation. The situation, on a hillslope with a terrace and stairways, adds greatly to the overall effect of the buildings.

Other things to be studied in Warwick are the excellent collections of local fossils and of British birds in the Museum in the Market Place, several good half-timbered houses, as Oken's House (in Castle Street), the house at the corner of New Street and Swan Street, &c.

**Mill Street and the Old Bridge.** —When approaching Warwick by the Leamington road, if we turn to the left instead of passing through the East Gate, we shall soon reach the entrance to the castle, beyond which Mill Street extends down to the river side. This street is unquestionably one of the most picturesque in England (figure 49)—its old

49 (OPPOSITE) MILL STREET, WARWICK.

houses, its curves, the ivy-covered cottage where it abuts on the river, and the splendid view it affords of Caesar's Tower, combine to form a series of pictures in which the history of the past seems brought before our very eyes. The Avon ripples by the lower end of Mill Street, and was formerly crossed here by a bridge, of which the stone piers still remain all ruinous and ivy covered.

Mill Street was one of very few roads to emerge completely unscathed from the devastating fire of 1694. It retains numerous excellent examples of timber-framed architecture and gives a good impression of what much of the rest of the town must have looked like before the Great Fire of 1694.

Here, too, is the castle mill, long disused, but helping to complete a scene which includes many elements of the rarest beauty.

In 1789 the old bridge, which linked the town of Warwick with the opposite bank of the river and which carried the main road to Banbury, was declared unsafe. It was a medieval structure, with fourteen arches. An Act of Parliament was obtained, giving powers to divert the main road 200 yards upstream, and to build a new bridge. This was opened in 1793, a daring and impressive structure with a single arch of 105 feet span. The old bridge was subsequently badly damaged in a flood which carried away most of the arches, but its picturesque vegetation-clad pillars remain to the present day.

**St. Mary's Church, with the Beauchamp Chapel.** —In the year 1694 a great misfortune befell the town of Warwick. A fire broke out which consumed the greater part of the town, and also most of the fine church of St. Mary, which had been rebuilt by the second Thomas Beauchamp in 1394. Fortunately the eastern part of the church was saved, and this

Rebuilding work on St Mary's after the fire of 1694 was largely paid for by public donations, including £11,000 from the town of Warwick itself, and £1,000 from Queen Anne. Sir Christopher Wren gave advice on the work, and the detailed supervision of se of the project was undertaken by Wren's master mason, Edward Strong. The architect inspiration behind the rebuilding was, however, Sir William Wilson, who rebuilt it in a contemporary interpretation of late Gothic style.

includes the choir or chancel, in the centre of which is the high tomb of the first Thomas Beauchamp, Earl of Warwick, and Katherine his countess (both died 1369). On the north of the chancel is the chapter house, which has been converted into a mausoleum for the huge tomb of Fulke Greville, the first Lord Brooke, who was murdered by his body servant in 1628. The inscription upon this tomb is well known—"Fulk Grevill, servant to Queen Elizabeth, counsellor to King James, and friend to Sir Philip Sidney".

Beneath the chancel is the oldest part of St. Mary's—the Norman crypt,—in which an ancient wooden ducking-stool is kept.

50
BEAUCHAMP
CHAPEL,
ST. MARY'S
CHURCH,
WARWICK.

But the gem of St. Mary's is the mortuary chapel placed on the south side of the chancel, and built in 1464 by the executors of Richard Beauchamp, eleventh Earl of Warwick. It lies much below the level of the rest of the church, and is

entered by a (restored) doorway adorned with the bear and ragged staff, which leads out of the east end of the south transept. The painted glass of the fine east window suffered very bad treatment during the Civil War, and the altar-piece beneath it dates only from 1735; but the chapel contains some magnificent tombs, of which that of the founder, Richard Beauchamp (who died at Rouen in 1439), occupies a central position, and is by far the finest. It consists of grey Purbeck marble, upon which rests a life size effigy of the earl in gilt brass; around the sides of the tomb are niches containing portrait-figures of members of the Beauchamp family (figure 50).

The Beauchamp Chapel miraculously survived the 1694 fire unscathed. This, with the very impressive crypt and the late fourteenth-century chancel, are the most significant remaining parts of the older church. It was in fact started in 1443, four years after the earl's death. The work proceeded very slowly: the chapel was not completed until 1464, and was not formally consecrated until 1475.

A little to the south-west of this grand central tomb stands a somewhat similar high tomb to Ambrose Dudley, the "good" Earl of Warwick, who died in 1589; and against the north wall of the chapel is the extremely ornate (but debased in style) monument of Robert Dudley, Earl of Leicester (died 1588), and his countess, Lettice (died 1634). At the south-east of the chapel is a curious monument to Dudley's deformed son—"the noble Impe, Robert of Dudley"—who died while little more than an infant.

On the north side of the Beauchamp Chapel a door gives access to a short flight of steps which leads to a small chantry chapel having a ceiling of exquisite fan-work.

After the fire of 1694, the tower and body of St. Mary's were rebuilt under the direction of Sir William Wilson. The proportions are good, and the effect from a distance is therefore pleasing, but the details of the work are poor and inartistic. At the latest "restoration", in 1896, the ugly side galleries were removed.

**Warwick Castle and its history.** —Many as are the beauties of the ancient capital of Warwickshire it must be agreed that they culminate in the grand and imposing edifice which, built on a rock overhanging the Avon, dominates the town today as it has done for the last six centuries.

Warwick Castle, 'the most perfect piece of castellated antiquity in the kingdom', is—like many great fortresses—the product of building work which has taken place over many centuries. Because it has long been a great house rather than a military fortress, it has undergone prolonged improvement and 'restoration', and especially in the eighteenth and nineteenth centuries much of what was constructed was designed in a fantasy of sham medieval style. This has added greatly to the magnificence of its appearance, and means that Warwick can show examples of almost all architectural styles from the 12th century to the nineteenth. There was 'Gothicisation' in the late eighteenth century, and far-reaching restoration in 1863–72. It was sold by Lord Brooke in 1978 to Pearson plc and is now part of the Tussaud's Group.

An exquisite general view of the castle and the river is obtained from the fine stone bridge over the Avon, built in 1790—a vista of trees and towers which is even better seen (figure 52) from the grounds of the Boating Club (reached by passing through an archway in Mill Street).

The gatehouse and entrance to the castle are situated in the top of Mill Street, and, passing through a cutting in the solid sandstone rock, we find ourselves in front of the barbican and gate-house, with Caesar's Tower (built 1360) on the left (figure 51) and Guy's Tower (1394) on the right. Passing by a modern bridge over the moat, and through the archway with its portcullis, we enter the courtyard, where peacocks scream and parade upon the grassy lawn. The great mound of earth upon which Ethelfleda is said to have built a tower in A.D. 915 is right in front of us; the entrance to the gardens (flanked by

51
CAESAR'S TOWER, WARWICK CASTLE.

The Bear Tower and the Clarence Tower were intended to be the turrets of a much larger tower, a project inherited by Richard III from his brother George, Duke of Clarence (son-in-law of the Earl of Warwick) but left unfinished on Richard's death at Bosworth in 1485.

Ethelflaeda was the daughter of King Alfred of Wessex. She married Ethelred of Mercia in 886, and on his death was recognised as Lady (i.e. Queen) of the Mercians. She led Mercia in its struggle against the Danes, and in the five years to 919 she founded a series of burhs, or fortified defended sites, as strongholds within her kingdom. One such burh was at Warwick, and probably occupied the same area as the medieval fortified town.

In a *cause célèbre* of 1977, Lord Brooke sold the vase to a consortium of London dealers, who in turn sold it to the Metropolitan Museum of Art, New York. An export licence was deferred, however, and when the purchase price of £253,808 was raised within the UK, the Warwick Vase became part of the Burrell Collection in Glasgow.

the unfinished Bear Tower and Clarence Tower) on the right; and the main mass of the castle buildings on the left, overlooking the Avon.

The castle contains some scanty Norman remains in the basement (used for domestic offices, &c.). The outer walls and towers are mainly the work of Thomas Beauchamp, about the end of the fourteenth century, while the large hall and other rooms, now inhabited by the Earl and Countess of Warwick, are of early seventeenth-century date. These latter rooms include many invaluable pictures, and magnificent collections of armour and of old furniture. Much damage was done by a fire in 1871.

The gardens are very beautiful, and contain the famous "Warwick Vase", found in 1770 at the bottom of a lake near Tivoli by Sir William Hamilton.

By a ferry it is possible to cross the Avon, and from the opposite (southern) side of the river the castle with its river front, and the grand cedars of Lebanon at its west end, are seen to great advantage.

**Guy's Cliffe, House, and Mill.** —A mile or so north of Warwick, and on the east side of the famous highway to Kenilworth and Coventry, stands the house of Guy's Cliffe (now the residence of Lord Algernon Percy). Here the soft red sandstone rock rises above a pool of the Avon, and contains a cave which, even in Saxon

times, was the favourite residence of a succession of hermits. Among these is reckoned the famous Guy, "Earl of Warwick", who, after a pilgrimage in the Holy land, is said to have retired to this lovely spot, and to have received alms daily from his wife Phillis (who quite failed to recognize him in the disguise which he assumed), but to whom he revealed himself a few days before his death. This story unfortunately rests upon no historical foundation. Guy's Cliffe House is visible from the road through a fine avenue of firs, and close at hand

52 WARWICK CASTLE. THE RIVER FRONT, FROM THE FERRY.

The site of Guy's Cliffe is impressive, with the Avon curving around the foot of a nearly-precipitous wooded slope, the 'Cliffe' of the name. Hermits lived here in the later medieval period, and in 1422–3 Richard Beauchamp, earl of Warwick, built a chapel which still survives. In 1751 the first part of the present house was constructed for Samuel Greatheed, M.P. for Coventry. It was greatly extended and altered by his son in the 1790s and again in 1818, and in the process became elaborately and fantastically Gothicised. This distinctly bizarre house has twice been damaged by fire and is now ruinous, overgrown, and dangerous.

is the famous Mill—"there has been a mill here for at least a thousand years"—with its wooden balcony dating from 1821 (figure 53).

On the opposite (left hand) side of the road is Blacklow Hill, where a monument erected in 1821 marks the spot where Piers Gaveston was executed, after a mock trial in the Great Hall of Warwick Castle, in 1312.

The present mill at Guy's Cliffe, now a restaurant, was built in the 1820s, incorporating some of the fabric of an older predecessor. The architectural detailing was 'Regency Gothick', in keeping with the prevailing taste and with the contemporary embellishment of the great house just up the river.

Piers Gaveston, the much-hated favourite of Edward II, was captured by his enemies at Scarborough in 1312. He was eventually brought to Warwick for trial, and summarily executed on Blacklow Hill. The monument to Gaveston includes the words 'The minion of a hateful king, in life and death a miserable instance of misrule'.

## CHAPTER IX

# The Castle of Kenilworth
# and the City of Coventry

"Far from the sun and summer gale,
In thy green lap was nature's darling laid,
What time, where luck Avon strayed,
To him the mighty mother did unveil
Her awful face: the dauntless child
Stretch'd forth his little arms, and smil'd.
—*Thomas Gray*, 1750

**enilworth and its Castle.**—Continuing our walk northwards from Guy's Cliffe we pass through the very pretty village of Leek Wootton (Hill Wootton, with even prettier thatched cottages—figure 54—lies less than a mile due east) and soon reach Kenilworth Castle, which is five miles north of Warwick, and one mile west of Kenilworth station (London and North-Western). The Norman keep of Kenilworth is much the oldest part of the structure, and was probably built by Geoffrey de Clinton, son of a De Clinton to whom the site was granted by Henry I in 1120. West of the Keep are the Kitchens and the Buttery, and then comes the Strong Tower (sometimes called Mervyn's Tower). On the south of the Strong Tower is the Banqueting-Hall, built by John of Gaunt; and east of this again are the White Hall, the Presence-Chamber, and, last of all, "Leicester's Buildings", erected by the earl in 1571 and now tottering to their fall (figure 55).

Ascending to the top of the Strong Tower we note the inner courtyard at our feet. The outer or Base Court includes a "pleasaunce" or garden on the north side, and is completely surrounded by a high and strong wall, placed along which, at intervals, are four towers. Outside this wall, to the west and

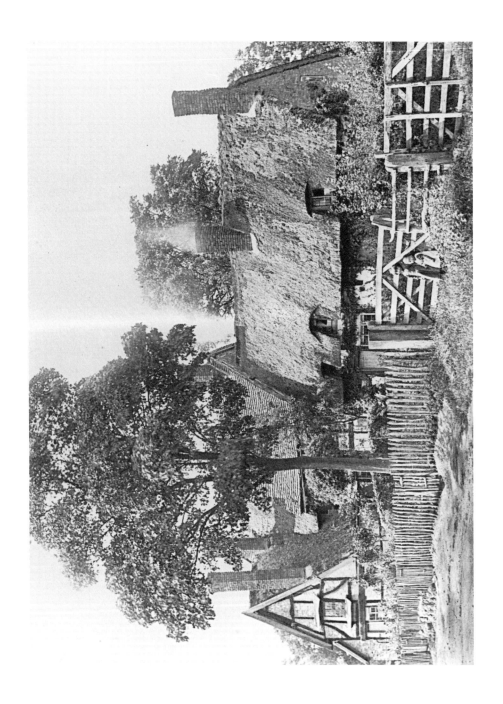

south, the low flat meadows indicate the position of the "Great Lake", which helped to protect the castle on those sides, while on the east there was a moat. The fine detached building near the entrance (now used as a dwelling-house) is Leicester's Gate House, and was built by Dudley in 1570; the low buildings against the wall to the south-east of this are the stables.

---

The splendid ruins of Kenilworth castle are one of the finest medieval monuments in England, and have been recognised as such for over three centuries. When Harrison wrote they were in some physical danger—he describes Leicester's Buildings as 'tottering to their fall'—but public guardianship under English Heritage and its predecessors has ensured that the ruins have been consolidated and made safe, landscaped and properly interpreted.

---

Kenilworth Castle was granted by Henry III to Simon de Montfort in 1254. It was besieged and taken by the king in 1266. In 1563 Elizabeth bestowed the castle upon her favourite, Robert Dudley, Earl of Leicester, and here she was entertained by him on several occasions, and notably with great magnificence in 1575. Cromwell gave the estate to certain of his officers, by whom it was partly dismantled and the lake drained. After the Restoration it became the property of the Hyde family, through whom it descended to the Earl of Clarendon, its present owner.

54 (OPPOSITE)
THATCHED
COTTAGES,
HILL
WOOTTON.

---

The situation of the castle has altered dramatically since the seventeenth century. It was formerly almost surrounded by a very large shallow lake (drained in the 1650s after the Civil War) which acted not only as a defence but also added scenic beauty once the castle became a residence. On this lake were performed many of the elaborate and fantastic pageants which greeted Elizabeth I when she came to Kenilworth to stay with Leicester in 1575.

---

It is interesting to remember that a later genius—Sir Walter Scott,—who much resembled Shakespeare in his rare combination of business capacity with literary ability, visited Kenilworth in 1820 to study the castle in connection with the

writing of the famous novel which bears its name. He stayed at the King's Arms Hotel.

**Kenilworth Church** (St. Nicholas) lies less than half a mile east of the castle. It most notable feature is a fine Norman doorway in the west front of the tower, which was taken in 1600 from the ruins of the adjacent priory. Of this priory, the remains of the gate house still stand at the west end of the churchyard, and its foundations have lately been uncovered.

> The house of the Augustinian canons at Kenilworth was founded by the same Geoffrey de Clinton who in 1125 began work on the castle. The priory was never large or prosperous, although it was upgraded to become an abbey in 1439. It was dissolved in 1539 and most of the buildings were soon demolished.

**The City of Coventry.** —"As the crow flies" Coventry is twenty miles north-east of Stratford-upon-Avon, and the same distance south-east of Birmingham. It is five miles north-east of Kenilworth, and for driving, cycling, or motoring perhaps

The Warwick–Coventry road (A429) is of course very different now. Scenically, the area has been greatly altered too—notably, the huge growth of Coventry since 1918 has swamped some of the northern end of the route with suburban development, although the tree-lined straight stretch from the outskirts of Kenilworth to Stivichall Common is still impressive.

there is no better or pleasanter road in England than the one from Warwick through Kenilworth to Coventry. The name of the city seems to be derived from the existence of a Saxon *convent* here, of which St. Osburg was the abbess when it was destroyed by Canute in 1016. Leofric, Earl of Mercia, is said to have founded a Benedictine monastery on the site of the ruined convent, but his name has come down to us chiefly on account of his countess, the famous Lady Godiva, whose memorable ride was recalled by Tennyson while he—

56
COVENTRY.
THE THREE
SPIRES.

"Waited for the train at Coventry,
  And hung with grooms and porters on the bridge,
    To watch the three tall spires."

This is the bridge which spans the line as we enter the precincts of the city when walking northwards from Kenilworth. Research fails to trace the legend of Godiva farther back than the fourteenth century, while it is certain that "Peeping Tom" is an addition made in Charles II's reign. In later times Coventry was the scene of the proposed encounter between the Dukes of Norfolk and of Hereford on Gosford Green in 1398, the story of which is related by Shakespeare in his *Richard II.* Elizabeth visited the city in 1565, and Mary Queen of Scots stayed at the Bull Inn as a prisoner in 1569. during the Civil War it was a Puritan stronghold, and as a punishment its walls were razed by order of Charles II.

Time, war and planning have ravaged Coventry, but the three spires are still the outstanding feature of its skyline. There is, however, little else that Harrison would recognise. In the early 1920s the ancient city began to grow rapidly, with the development of the bicycle and motor industries. By the late 1930s Coventry was England's fastest-growing city, and the previously small and well-defined built-up area was sprawling outwards as great new suburbs sprang up. The city centre had been of exceptional historic interest—it was one of the finest medieval cities in Europe, of remarkable architectural quality and with many streets of great beauty. Unfortunately these areas, which would now be regarded as a priceless asset and a national treasure, were then seen as hopelessly old-fashioned, and not in keeping with the city's modern image. Between 1936 and 1939 great swathes of the medieval city were laid waste in order to build new streets suitable for motor traffic—the demolition, in 1935-6, of the same Butcher Row area which was commended by Harrison, was the greatest vandalism of all, for here was an almost untouched medieval quarter. During the 1940 air raids the Luftwaffe continued the destruction: much of the remainder of the city centre was flattened, hundreds of people were killed, and the medieval parish church of St Michael (since 1918 the cathedral) was gutted. After the war the rebuilding work began, and the pioneering traffic-free city centre constructed—but, as David McGrory, the city's most recent historian, points out, the replanning meant that most of the remaining medieval heritage was destroyed. In 1946 there were some 350 buildings in Coventry dating from before 1700, but in 1966 only 34 of these survived.

**A walk through Coventry.** —Entering Coventry from the south, by the Kenilworth and Warwick road, we note the "three tall spires" of Christ Church, Holy Trinity, and St.

57
FORD'S
HOSPITAL,
COVENTRY.

Michael, the two latter being in close proximity. Passing through the nicely laid out gardens of "Greyfriars' Green", we turn to the right, and find ourselves in Greyfriars' Street, where stands Ford's Hospital, a most picturesque wooden building, erected by William Ford in 1529 as a home for indigent old women (figure 57). Continuing up Greyfriars' Street, and turning to the left, we reach the very centre of Coventry, where a wooden image known as "Peeping Tom" looks down upon all and sundry from an upper window of

103

A new road now covers most of Greyfriars Green, but Ford's Hospital is still extant. It was founded in 1509 under the terms of the will of William Ford, a merchant in the wool and cloth trades which were the foundation of the prosperity of the medieval city. Further endowments were made in 1517 and 1529—originally the hospital housed men and women, but by 1700 only women were being admitted. The inmates were to be 'of good name and fame, and...of good honesty...decayed and come to poverty and great need, in the same city'. On the night of 14 October 1940 the warden, a nurse and six of the inmates were killed when the hospital was wrecked in an air raid. Between 1950 and 1953 the fabric was painstakingly restored, using salvaged timbers from all over the city. The result is a triumph of craftsmanship—the building today is scarcely distinguishable from that in Harrison's photograph.

the "King's Head". There are several fine old half-timbered and gabled houses still to be seen in the streets of Coventry, and two "gates" of the ancient walls in Cook Street and in Hales Street; while Butcher's Row is an old-world bit indeed. But the most remarkable building in the city is unquestionably St. Mary's Hall, in Bailey Lane, facing St. Michael's Church. This edifice, completed in 1414, was the hall of the famous Guilds of Coventry. Of the many objects of interest which it contains perhaps the chief is a grand tapestry intended to commemorate a visit paid to the city by Henry VI and Queen Margaret in 1451.

The great hall of St Mary, with St Michael's church the finest of all the medieval buildings of old Coventry, is the most remarkable survivor. The bombs rained all around it in 1940, and the cathedral opposite was devastated, but the superb medieval hall survived the bombs and fires even though parts of the building were damaged. Harrison would at least recognise this, even if almost everything else would seem totally unfamiliar—of all the places in this book, it is Coventry which has changed the most since his day.

**The Mystery Plays.** —During the Middle Ages Coventry was famous for the performance of pageants and religious or "mystery" plays in the streets of the city under the direction of the Grey Friars. After the dissolution of the monasteries the plays were still kept up by the members of the local guilds, and were not finally suppressed until 1580. Our Shakespeare would then be a lad of sixteen, and some of the references in *Hamlet* [§] and other of his works make it probable that he had, indeed, "seen Herod rage" in the streets of Coventry.

§ *Hamlet,* act iii, sc. 2: "It out-herods Herod."

The Coventry mystery plays have been the subject of extensive research in recent years, as interest in early English drama and music has grown. Two plays survive: those of the guild of the weavers, and of the shearmen and tailors. Others were known, but are now lost. The last complete performance took place in 1579, thirty years after the dissolution of the guilds which had originally performed them. They were abolished despite their great fame and the pressure for their survival exerted by the city council. Fortunately, however, the text of these two was preserved, and in 1817–36 they were edited, published, and made available to posterity, by Thomas Sharp, a local antiquary.

## CHAPTER X

# Wanderings in the Forest of Arden

"Avon, thy rural view, thy pastures wild,
The willows that o'erhang thy twilight edge,
Their boughs entangling with the embattled sedge;
Thy brink with watery foliage quaintly fring'd,
Thy surface with reflected verdure ting'd;
Soothe me with many a pensive pleasure mild."
—*Thomas Warton,* 1777.

**ampton-in-Arden.** —The name of Hampton-in-Arden tells of its former state as a village situated in a clearing of the great Midland Forest. It lies half-way between Birmingham and Kenilworth, and had a station on the London and North-Western line.

> The rural village of Hampton-in-Arden now lies at the heart of the English transport network. The M6 is three miles north, the M42 half a mile west, the main London–Birmingham railway line cuts through the village, the National Exhibition Centre is two miles away, and the runway of Birmingham International Airport points like an arrow at Hampton. Harrison's peaceful world is no more!

The church has Norman piers in the nave, and the chancel is partly Norman; the rest of the building being Perpendicular with embattled nave and tower. Note the very ancient stone seat in the south aisle, and the "Heart Shrine" in the south wall of the chancel. This formerly contained the heart of a Knight Templar enclosed in a silver case. West of and close to the church is an old stone manor house,

> The building just west of the church is the timber-framed fifteenth and sixteenth century manor house; the stone manor house, to the north west, is a very good fake medieval building of the 1870s, built for Sir Frederick Peel, son of the prime minister Sir Robert Peel.

58
THE MARSH
BRIDGE,
HAMPTON-IN-
ARDEN.

now a farmhouse, which formerly belonged to the Arden family.

The River Blythe runs one mile south-east of Hampton, and is here crossed by the ancient "Marsh Bridge" (figure 58), one of the "pack horse" bridges, and probably four or five centuries old. The railway bridge crosses the stream a few yards lower down, and the contrast is great indeed!

The packhorse bridge at Bradnocks Marsh is still to be seen: it is a five-arched bridge with a cross base on the eastern pier, and it probably dates from the late fourteenth or early fifteenth centuries. The bridge, 77 feet long and only 5 feet wide, was almost demolished in 1891: only the pleading of the Birmingham Archaeological Society saved it.

From Hampton it is a delightful walk of three miles in a south-easterly direction to another pretty village, that of Berk-swell, which derives its name from the fine spring of water that still rises into a great stone cistern at the east end of the churchyard. Here, too, is the village green, which boasts a well-preserved pair of stocks.

It is still possible to walk from Hampton-in-Arden to Berkswell, although a dual carriageway cuts across the route at the halfway point: Berkswell is surprisingly unspoiled considering its position between Birmingham and Coventry. The cistern and the stocks on the green, and the attractive church, are little altered from Harrison's day. The cistern, fed by powerful springs, was restored by public subscription in 1851, and supplied most of the water for the village until piped supplies were installed in the 1940s. The stocks have five holes; stories abound that this was because they were specially made for a one-legged man, but the real reason is said, more prosaically, to be that there were originally six holes but wood around the last one rotted away.

The church of St. John the Baptist is one of the most interesting in Warwickshire. The crypt is partly Saxon, partly Norman; the nave and aisles are Early English and Decorated; while the clerestory, tower and porch are of the seventeenth century. The half timbered gabled south porch (figure 59) is extremely picturesque, and has an upper story.

The churchyard cross retains the original base, but the shaft is of recent date.

Although it is doubtful if the church has any Anglo-Saxon fabric, there remains the strong possibility that the parts of the unique octagonal east end of the crypt may be built on an Anglo-Saxon base. The chancel and the crypt itself are Norman, and the delightful two-storeyed timber porch is from the late fifteenth or early sixteenth centuries.

**Henley-in-Arden.** —This quaint little town claims a remote antiquity, dating back to the time when it was but a collection of Saxon huts in a forest clearing. Then came the Norman knight, De Montfort, and built a castle on the hill in the twelfth century; but of this castle only mounds and ditches remain.

59
CHURCH PORCH, BERKSWELL.

60
CHURCH AND
STREET,
HENLEY-IN-
ARDEN.

There may have been a minor settlement at Henley itself in the Saxon period, but the town is in essence a very good example of a planned medieval new town. It was laid out in the twelfth century as a single long main street with regularly spaced burgage plots on either side. The situation of the town, on the road north from Stratford (itself a new town of the same period) to Birmingham, was favourable to its commercial potential. The market cross is probably fifteenth century: the head is now lost, but it is recorded that in the 1890s it had four sides with scenes depicting the rood, the Trinity, St Peter and his key and (probably) the Virgin and Child. The Guild Hall was extensively restored in 1915, having been previously used as shops. It, too, dates from the fifteenth century, as do several other attractive inns and town houses including the Old George and the Blue Bell.

Henley now consists of one long street, near the centre of which stands the much weathered Market Cross and the church (Perpendicular), together with some old houses (figure 60) one of which (near the cross) was the hall of the local guild. The lane next to the parish church leads to the adjoining church of Beaudesert, which had a Norman chancel, chancel arch, and south door. Henley has of late years been connected by a branch line with the Great Western Railway at Lapworth station; and this, with the advent of motor and cycle, has done something to wake up, but at the same time to destroy much of the charm of this sleepy old town.

Beaudesert is the oldest part of the settlement at Henley—the original village which was later superseded by the new town on the main road. The fact that the church is partly Norman points to the antiquity of the community, and is in contrast to Henley, where the parish church is entirely fifteenth century in date. The complex of castle mounds at Beaudesert is also Norman. The railway line linking Henley with Lapworth, which was new when Harrison as writing, was one of the least successful of all English branch lines: it opened in June 1894, and closed on New Year's Day 1915, after a working life of only 21 years. In the meantime, in 1907, the direct line from Birmingham to Stratford via Henley had opened—having survived threats of closure in the 1960s and 1970s this line survives as an increasingly busy commuter route.

**Wootton Wawen.** —From Henley-in-Arden a road leads southwards for two miles to the "Woodtown of Wagen", now the village of Wootton Wawen, but a thousand years ago the property of one Wagen, a Saxon chief. The church here (figure 61) is famous in that the two lower stages of the central tower are Saxon, with very narrow arches. The interior includes a large chantry chapel, and there are tombs of the Harewells (fifteenth and sixteenth centuries), and of William Somerville (1742), the author of *The*

Harrison noted that the two lower stages of the tower of Wootton Wawen church were pre-Conquest. He thought they were 'Saxon' although later architectural descriptions use the term 'Anglo-Danish'. Part of the nave dates from the 12th century, and there is excellent later medieval work. This is unquestionably one of the most impressive and interesting parish churches in Warwickshire.

*Chase* and other well known poems; a fine old oak chest, and a row of chained books are also worthy of notice.

### Kinwarton and its Dove-Cot. —Aston

Cantlow is a long two miles south of Wootton Wawen, and the road then turns westward, parallel to the little branch railway which connects Bearley with Alcester. Passing through Great Alne, with its thatched post office hemmed in by box hedges and embosomed in flowering creepers, we make a slight detour to the small hamlet of Kinwarton. Here there is a tiny church but a very large stone dove-cot. Such dove-cots are relics of the time when the right to keep pigeons was possessed only by the lord of the manor. They were built to afford nesting places for hundreds of pairs of birds, whose flesh was considered no small delicacy.

62
STONE
DOVE-COT,
KINWARTON.

The little branch railway which connected Bearley with Alcester has long gone, and housing estates have crept eastwards from Alcester, but Kinwarton is still a tiny and unspoiled hamlet beside the River Alne. Its massive dovecot can be dated by the detail of the ogee door arch to the early or mid-fourteenth century: it has over 500 nesting holes and is now owned by the National Trust. The church is only 57 feet long. It was rebuilt in 1316, and has a small weatherboarded bell turret of the sixteenth or seventeenth centuries.

### Alcester: once a Roman Station. —Another mile finds us

in Alcester town, where the Alne joins the Arrow, the latter stream running due south to mingle its waters with those of the Avon at Salford Priors. The Town Hall here (figure 63) dates back to 1641, and the lower part was formerly open and used as a market, but it was enclosed in modern times, and is now the county court. Alcester is one of the few places in

61 (OPPOSITE)
WOOTTON
WAWEN
CHURCH FROM
THE NORTH.

For over 200 years Alcester was known to have been a Roman town, but it is only since the mid–1950s that serious archaeological investigation has taken place. This has shown that the settlement was more substantial than had previously been thought, and it is now believed that ALAVNA was an important local market centre, at the junction of the east-west road (Droitwich-Stratford) with the north-south route now known as Ryknield Street. The area of the Roman town included the modern town centre, and it seems to have had earthwork defences although it was never walled. The town hall is probably older than Harrison suggests—a date of 1618 is now thought more likely, although it is known that the fine hammerbeam roof of the upper chamber does date from 1641. As Harrison says, the six arches of the lower floor were originally completely open, and the space was used as a market, but they were subsequently filled in.

Warwickshire which can be identified with the Roman occupation. It stands on the Ryknield Street, as was the Roman station called *Alauna*. Later on there was a monastery here, but if it no trace remains. The church of St. Nicholas has a fine tower (Decorated): but the rest was rebuilt in the eighteenth century. It contains marble statues by Chantrey and by Count Gleichen, and the high tomb of Sir Fulke Greville (died 1559) and his wife.

Alcester parish church has a fine tower, with thirteenth-century work below and fifteenth century above, but the nave and aisles were constructed in Classical style in 1729–30, apparently after a fire or other structural problem. The east end was rebuilt in 1870–1. Although Sir Fulke Greville and his wife Elizabeth died in 1559, their tomb, described by Wedgwood as 'not as skilful as some but as forceful as any', was not erected until 1665.

63 (OPPOSITE)
TOWN HALL,
ALCESTER.

**Alvechurch and Needle-Land.** —When returning from Alcester by the Midland Railway, it is worth while to break the journey at Alvechurch (ten miles farther north), if only to stroll for an hour in the churchyard, where ancient yews of unknown antiquity cast heavy shadows, and where the rooks have established themselves in great numbers in the fine elms which encircle "God's acre".

The valley of the Arrow may be styled "Needle-Land". At Alcester, Alvechurch, Studley, and, most important of all, Redditch, countless numbers of needles are manufactured annually, together with fish hooks and fishing tackle.

Studley is still a rural industrial centre—not quite a town, but more than a village—and the needle-making industry, although now very much reduced in scale, still continues in the Arrow valley. The industry seems to have started in Studley, and it was flourishing there and in adjacent villages by the middle of the seventeenth century. It was at the height of its importance in the mid nineteenth century—in 1851 over one-third of the adult population of Studley were employed in the trade. Needle-making in Alcester, the southernmost outpost of what was in many ways a far-flung corner of the Black Country metalworking industries, was dying out by the end of the nineteenth century.

## CHAPTER XI

# More wanderings in Arden

"William Shakespeare, the glory of the English stage;
whose nativity at Stratford-upon-Avon is the highest
honour that town can boast of."
—*Edward Phillips,* 1675.

 **he Centre of England.** —Since Michael Drayton, the friend of Shakespeare, writes of Warwickshire as "That shire which we the heart of England well may call", it is but natural that we should expect to find somewhere in the county a spot which may be defined as "the centre of England"; and it is also natural that there should be several claimants for this distinction. Of course there is really no exact spot of which the fact can be affirmed with scientific certainty, for much depends upon how and whence the measurements are taken; but the contest lies chiefly between a fine old oak near Leamington and the village market cross of Meriden (figure 71).

Meriden village is three miles east of Hampton-in-Arden, and about the same distance south of Maxstoke Priory. The cross has unfortunately been removed from its former site, though only to the other end of the village. The church of

Meriden is not only the centre of England—it is midway between Birmingham and Coventry, and in the twentieth century it suffered greatly from motor traffic. The A45 was one of the busiest and most congested trunk roads of England in the years before the construction of the motorway network, and Meriden was ravaged by heavy traffic. The building of a bypass in 1959 eased the problem, as did the construction of the M6 ten years later, and the village has become rather more tranquil of late. The watershed between the Avon and Tame catchments lies about three-quarters of a mile south-east of the church, where tiny tributaries of the two rivers, no more than ditches, do indeed connect.

St. Lawrence here (restored 1883) includes some Norman portions, with much later and modern work. The villagers of Meriden adduce an argument which they think proves the centrality of the village, in the fact that after heavy rains the water in a local pond discharges itself in two directions northwards into the Tame and so to the Trent and North Sea, and southwards into the Avon and thence to the Bristol Channel.

64
VILLAGE
CROSS,
MERIDEN.

**Balsall Street and the Village Smithy.** —The three great railway lines (the Great Western, the Midland, and the London and North-Western) which run from Birmingham southwards through Shakespeare-Land, present great advantages to the lovers of country walks, because it is possible to travel by one line and then—the lines lying from four to six miles apart—walk across and return by another to the starting place (Birmingham, Stratford-upon-Avon, or Warwick) without having to retrace one's steps or go over the same ground twice.

> The three great railway lines which Harrison describes still exist: today they are respectively the lines from Birmingham Snow Hill to Leamington and Oxford; from Birmingham New Street to Worcester; and from New Street to Coventry. The possibility of country walks from station to station has been much reduced, because so much of the intervening area has been developed for housing and new roads: Knowle, which was a small country village, is now, with Dorridge, a substantial town. No longer are there blacksmiths and wheelwrights at Balsall Street, and nearby Balsall Common is part of a sprawling and rather undistinguished dormitory suburb.

65
THE VILLAGE
SMITHY,
BALSALL.

A very pleasant walk of this kind is to cross from Berkswell station (London and North-Western) to Knowle station (Great Western), taking Balsall Street and Temple Balsall on the way: or, of course, the reverse direction may be taken.

66
THE MASTER
BLACKSMITH.

Three of the places just named we have already described, and in figure 65 we give an illustration of the blacksmith's smithy and wheelwright's shop at the hamlet of Balsall Street, one mile west of Berkswell station. And, having persuaded the master blacksmith to come to the door, we are also able to present a type (figure 66) of the Warwickshire working man of the present day—a type which had changed surprisingly little since Will Shakespeare wrote lovingly in *The Taming of the Shrew* of "Stephen Sly and old John Naps of Greece (an obvious misprint for Greet, a common Warwickshire place-name), and Peter Turf, and Henry Pimpernell", while he evidently had a warm corner in his heart even for "Christopher Sly, old Sly's son of Burton-heath", and for "Marian Hacket, the fat ale-wife of Wincot".

### The Ancient Town of Coleshill.

—Coleshill—a favourite resort of the busy workers of Birmingham—is eight miles east

of that city, and one mile south of Forge Mills station, on the Midland line. Walking southwards from the railway station we cross the River Cole (which runs northwards to join the Tame) by a good medieval bridge, beyond which the little town is seen rising, its height capped by the fine spire (rebuilt 1887) of the church of St. Peter and St. Paul, whose architecture is partly Decorated, partly Perpendicular.

Climbing the hill by the main street we find ourselves in the market place, where may be seen a combination of those terrors to evil-doers, formerly in common use in England, the pillory, stocks, and whipping post. Some of the iron work is old, but the greater part of this structure is so evidently new that it must be among the very latest put up in this country.

67
NORMAN FONT,
COLESHILL
CHURCH.

The problems which have faced other towns and villages in the belt of country between Birmingham and Coventry have also affected Coleshill. A century ago, as Harrison suggests, Birmingham workers went to Coleshill for a day out. Then came cars, power stations and industrial development. The old coaching town was overwhelmed with traffic, until the bypass was completed in 1939—a road which, today, has a curiously historic look of its own, for it was one of the earliest major bypass roads. The town is much battered, and there has been a great deal of demolition and redevelopment since the 1940s, but plenty of older buildings survive—as do the pillory, whipping post, stocks and manacles mentioned by Harrison.

The church stands close by, and in the interior we note the tombs of two of the Clintons (the first possessors of the manor) and of several of their successors, the Digbys, including Simon Digby (1519) and John Digby (1558). But the gem of the church is the large Norman font (figure 67), one of the best examples to be found in England.

**Maxstoke Priory and Castle.** —From Coleshill it is a pleasant walk of between three and four miles south-eastward to the ruins of Maxstoke Priory, crossing the pretty little River Blythe *en route*. This priory was built in 1336 by William de Clinton for the Order of St. Augustine. The ruins include an interesting gateway and gate house (now partly incorporated with a farmhouse), behind which is the central tower of the church, and some remains of the infirmary, &c. (figure 68).

From the priory we can readily reach Whitacre station (rather less than four miles to the north-west), taking Maxstoke Castle on the way. This building (figure 69) is a remarkably fine specimen of a fourteenth century fortified house. An

69
MAXSTOKE
CASTLE FROM
THE
SOUTH-EAST.

avenue of elms leads through a deer park to the castle, which is built in the form of a parallelogram, with a tower at each corner, the whole being surrounded by a moat. It was protected by the same William de Clinton as built the priory.

Maxstoke is unexpectedly remote. Its position off the east-west or north-south road axes, and away from the main railway lines, helped to preserve its isolation. The remarkable castle, built in the 1340s, was substantially altered in the early seventeenth century by Thomas (later Sir Thomas) Dilke, who acquired it in 1599. It is still in private ownership and is little altered since Harrison's day, retaining the atmosphere of romantic ruins so familiar to the Victorians.

**Arley Church and Street.** —Arley village is rather more than a mile north of its railway station (Midland), and deserves a visit if only to study the charming combination offered by the tower of the ancient church of St. Wilfrid with the houses

123

of its single street. The church is Early Decorated, and contains a fifteenth century monument of a priest, and some still earlier painted glass.

> Arley was a quiet country village until 1901, when work began on sinking a new colliery a mile to the south. The first coal was raised in the autumn of 1902, and the mine grew rapidly. New Arley, a community of red-brick houses, began to grow next to the mine, and this soon eclipsed Old Arley in size and population. The colliery reached its peak production in the 1930s and was closed in the late 1960s. The village of New Arley is currently being upgraded and improved. Meanwhile, Old Arley, with its eighteenth-century cottages and medieval church, remains comparatively untouched. The monument to a priest in the church dates from about 1350—he is recumbent with two angels at his pillow.

**Chesterton and its Windmill.** —Chesterton is an easy walk of three miles south-west from Southam Road and Harbury station, on the Great Western Railway. The geologist will first desire to inspect the extensive limestone quarries in the Lower Lias near Harbury; and the village church with its Early English tower is worth a glance. At Chesterton the very interesting church of St. Giles contains the monuments and busts of the Peyto family, including Sir William Peyto (died 1609), Sir Edward Peyto (died 1643), and Humphrey Peyto (died 1585).

> The quarries at Harbury began on a small scale in the late eighteenth century, but their period of major expansion came in the 1850s, after the opening of the railway line from Oxford to Birmingham. The improved transport links allowed a major industry to develop, producing blue lias for use in the local cement industry: large cement works were constructed at Rugby and Long Itchington. In the late 1920s there was a further period of expansion, as

About half a mile north-west of Chesterton church stands a very fine stone windmill, built by Sir Edward Peyto from the designs of Inigo Jones in 1632. It has six semicircular arches and a revolving roof covered with lead (figure 70).

70
STONE
WINDMILL,
CHESTERTON.

Some time back a ruinous building at Newport, Rhode Island (United States), was considered by certain Scandinavian antiquaries, and by others (including the poet Longfellow, who embodied his belief in a ballad—*The Skeleton in Armour*), as proving the discovery of America by the Danes in the twelfth century. Careful research, however, has shown that the Newport tower is but a copy of Chesterton mill, having been built by a Chesterton man—one Benedict Arnold—who emigrated in 1635.

There is a grand view from the windmill, and just at the northern foot of the hill upon which it stands is visible the rectangular outline of a Roman camp, placed upon the Roman road called the Fosse-way.

> The extraordinary windmill stands on the top of a prominent hill a mile north-west of the church. In an article in Warwickshire History (1971) E. G. Baxter dates the mill to 1632–5, noting that it replaced a watermill near the 'village' of Chesterton, and was evidently designed to be as visible and eyecatching as possible. There is no documentary record of a connection with Inigo Jones, and the name of the designer is unknown, but Jones' work clearly provided the inspiration for the project. The Mill House is also unlikely to have been the work of Inigo Jones, and probably dates from about 1660—Baxter notes that it was possibly not purpose-built, and it is certainly exceedingly grand for the purpose. As Harrison indicates, north-west of the windmill, straddling the Fosse Way, are earthworks of the small Roman fort and town of Chesterton. This was partly-excavated in 1923, and again in the 1960s.

The water mill and bridge on the southern side of the hill are also the work of Inigo Jones.

> Chesterton is a very strange place. It lies near the Fosse Way south-east of Leamington, and used to be very remote—although in the late 1980s the building of the M40 only a mile away somewhat reduced that isolation. It is a deserted medieval village, with few surviving buildings apart from the church, the millhouse and a couple of farms. The great mansion of the Peyto family, which formerly stood here, was pulled down in the early nineteenth century: Wedgwood says that at this time 'it lost its heart'. The church is mainly 13th century, and has not been much improved, which is by no means a misfortune in a Warwickshire church.

**The Home of the Comptons.** —Compton Wyniates, the delightful seat of the Marquess of Northampton, is twelve miles south-east of Stratford-upon-Avon, but is most commonly reached by driving eight miles westwards from Banbury. The grand red brick mansion lies so low that it is locally

known as "Compton in the Hole", and the suddenness of its appearance is invariably a matter of surprise to those who visit it for the first time (figure 71). It was built by Sir William Compton early in the reign of Henry VIII (c. 1510). Parts of the original moat still remain. The brickwork chimneys are most elaborate, while in the interior the great hall, with its roof of open timber work and minstrels' gallery, and the numerous secret passages and "hiding holes", invite and repay inspection.

CHAPTER XII

# The Eight
# "Shakespearean Villages"

"May Spring with purple flowers perfume thy urn;
And Avon with his green thy grave adorn;
Be all thy faults, whatever faults there be,
Imputed to the times, and not to thee."

—*E. Fenton,* 1711

F course *all* the villages within the area of Shake-speare-Land may be supposed to have been more or less frequently visited by the poet, and may therefore be more or less intimately connected with his name. But the title of "the Shakespearean Villages" has in some way come to be more or less specially associated with a certain group of eight; two of which—Pebworth and Long Marston—are situated on the south-east or Gloucester side of the Avon, while the other six—Hillborough, Grafton, Ex-hall, Wixford, Broom, and Bidford—lie close together in Warwickshire, on the north-west side of the river.

As a result of the boundary changes of 1931, Pebworth was transferred to Worcestershire, while Long Marston was included within Warwickshire.

**The Legend of Shakespeare's Crab Tree.** —Six miles south-west of Stratford, and about a mile before reaching Bidford village, a small crab apple tree is seen in a field on the left hand (nearly opposite a red brick barn on the other side of the road). This claims to be a descendant of the tree under which Shakespeare is locally

The drinking story is perhaps the most fantastic of all the legends and myths which have grown up around the name of William Shakespeare. The original crab apple tree is said to have been felled in the 1820s, and today 'Shake-speare's tree' is no longer a landmark.

said to have "slept the clock round" after a drinking match in which a band of gallants from Stratford had been woefully worsted by the "Sippers" of Bidford. The view from this point is very fine, and, after the defeated bard had stretched himself and looked around him, he is said to have pointed out the eight villages we have just mentioned (all of which are within sight), and summed up their peculiarities in the following lines:

> "Piping Pebworth: Dancing Marston:
> Haunted Hillborough: Hungry Grafton:
> Dodging Exhall: Papist Wixford:
> Beggarly Broom, and Drunken Bidford."

This legend first appears in print in the *British Magazine* for June 1762, and in later years was improved by the addition that the topers slept the Sunday over, so that Shakespeare was led to reprove a boy whom he saw ploughing on the Monday morning for his supposed desecration of the Sabbath!

It is possible to make the round of the eight villages from Stratford in a day's drive of about thirty miles; but it is needless to say that such a hasty visit is not to be recommended save as an "introduction" to the group. It is better to devote one day to the two villages (Marston and Pebworth) on the Gloucestershire side of the Avon; a second day may be well spent at Wixford, Exhall, and Grafton, which will leave Hillborough, Bidford, and Broom for a third day's work.

> When Harrison refers to driving he is thinking not of motoring but of travel in a pony-and-trap. Therefore his drives are very considerably more leisurely than those of the motorist in the 1990s.

**"Dancing" Marston.** —The very pretty village of Long Marston or Marston Sicca (*i.e. dry*, from its easily parched soil) is situated on the Great Western line, seven miles southwest of Stratford. The Church of St. James is a stone building (Perpendicular), whose register dates from 1651; it was partly restored in 1869.

The villagers here were—and indeed still are—famous for their skill as morris dancers, and were formerly wont at festive seasons to give exhibitions of their skill in all the country round. It is probable that they took part in the Kenilworth festivities before Queen Elizabeth in 1575. The village abounds in thatched cottages of the most picturesque type, but special notice should be taken of a good stone house which stands near the church, and which the rustics call "the Old King Charles' House", although its proper title is "King's Lodge". It was here that Charles II, disguised as a serving-man, found a temporary refuge during his flight from Worcester in 1651, and where his ignorance as to the use of a roasting-jack nearly led to his discovery. The house is now, as it was then, in the possession of the good old family of Tomes. The "jack" is kept in a glass case, and is willingly shown to visitors.

Although the village of Long Marston is still quite attractive its setting was drastically altered during the Second World War by the construction of a huge military depot, covering more than a square mile, just to the south. The railway station has now closed and the track (from Honeybourne to Stratford) is lifted—at present it is used as a cycle route and footpath, but there is a continuing campaign to reopen it as a railway. There is no evidence to support the view that the local dancers were present at Kenilworth, but they certainly visited the various Shakespeare celebrations in Stratford during the nineteenth century. Like the stories associated with Shakespeare, the tale of Charles II hiding in King's Lodge received later embroidering: in one version the king was boxed round the ears because of his incompetence in managing the roasting jack.

**"Piping" Pebworth.** —From Long Marston it is a pleasant two mile walk westwards to Pebworth. Notice how many of the houses and walls here are built of the thin-bedded blue lias limestone, the surface of the stone being often covered with fossil oysters. Pebworth had a fourteenth century church, to which several alterations and additions have been made, so that the architecture is now best described as "mixed". It contains a curious wall painting dated 1629, in memory of the Martin family. A good stone dove-cot stands in a field

72
PEBWORTH
CHURCH FROM
THE
SOUTH-EAST.

near the village; roses climb over and about the old tomb-stones in the churchyard, and the grey houses in the straggling street; while pear-trees occur in every hedge. From Pebworth it is but a two mile walk southwards to Honeybourne station (Great Western Railway), which stands exactly on the line of the Roman road called Ryknield Street; or in a northerly direction Bidford may be reached in five miles by passing through the charming villages of Dorsington and Barton.

Pebworth, as noted above, was once in Gloucestershire but was then transferred to Worcestershire. The county boundaries in this area were the most confused and intricate in England, with the four counties—Warwickshire, Worcestershire, Gloucestershire and Oxfordshire—intermingled and tangled. The tidy official minds of the 1920s decided that this could not continue (it undoubtedly did make administration very difficult) and in 1931 the whole area was reorganised. Honeybourne station, on the line from Oxford to Worcester, was closed in the 1960s but reopened twenty years later after a lengthy campaign by local residents.

**"Papist" Wixford.** —The village of Wixford stands on the east side of the River Arrow, the railway station (Midland) being on the other side of the stream, which here affords

73
THE VILLAGE
STREET,
WIXFORD.

excellent fishing. The small church of St. Milburg is chiefly Early English and Perpendicular, with north and south Norman doorways. In the churchyard there is a very fine yew tree, and also the base of a fourteenth century cross. The "street" of Wixford slopes westward down to the river, and includes some interesting stone cottages with thatched roofs (figure 82).

The name "papist", as applied to this village, is clearly due to the fact that it had always belonged to a Roman Catholic family.

> The peace of Wixford is now shattered by the recent construction of the A46 from Alcester to Evesham, following the line of the old railway between the two towns. The road crosses the river Arrow at the western end of the village street. The yew tree commented upon by Harrison was a famous landmark, and many legends grew up around it: allegedly the rector in the late 1660s wanted to fell it, but was prevented from doing so after local people petitioned the bishop of Worcester.

**"Dodging" Exhall.** This tiny village lies only half a mile east of Wixford. Its prefatory adjective is sometimes written "Dadging" or "Dudging"—a cant term implying begging proclivities in its inhabitants. But if taken as "Dodging", it probably refers to its out of the way and somewhat inaccessible position. The

74
CHURCH OF
ST. GILES,
EXHALL.

Church of St. Giles is Perpendicular, with a bricked-up Norman doorway on the north side. It was restored (neither "wisely" nor "well") in 1863 (figure 74). In the chancel are brasses to John Walsingham (died 1566) and his wife.

Exhall is still a small and secluded village. The church is a strange architectural hodge-podge. The Norman nave has very unusual square-headed windows of about 1320. In 1862–3, despite the vehement protests of the Worcester Diocesan Archaeological Society, the ill-advised 'restoration' so condemned by Harrison involved the bricking-up of a fine Norman doorway and other ancient windows, and the replacement of a medieval bell turret. In the photograph the stark contrast between old and new work can be very clearly seen. Note the hay-making in progress on the village green.

**"Hungry" Grafton.** —Temple Grafton—the "Hungry" Grafton of the rhyme—is rather more than a mile east of Exhall, and is approached from the latter village through its "suburb" of Arden's Grafton. The lane scenes about here are often of entrancing beauty, the branches of the trees arching over the roads and forming a natural framework for the rustic

cots of the villagers (figure 75). The term "hungry" is often applied by farmers to dry, poor land, to which large quantities of manure may be applied with but little apparent effect. The modern church is in the Decorated style, and was erected upon the site of a pre-existing church (which had fallen into ruins) in 1875. There is some reason for thinking that it was in the old church of Temple Grafton that William Shakespeare married Anne Hathaway; but the parish registers, unfortunately, only begin in 1693. From Grafton it is a pleasant walk of five or six miles eastwards through Binton, with its disused stone quarries, to Stratford-upon-Avon, while Bidford station lies only a mile to the south.

75
LANE AT
ARDEN'S
GRAFTON.

Like Exhall, the two Graftons have managed to retain their remote character, and the rural charm of the area remains. The dry, harsh, hungry land of the area was a consequence of its underlying rock: the district has beds of rather poor quality limestone, and in the eighteenth and nineteenth centuries this was extensively worked in shallow pits and quarries—the fields are still noticeably stony. The story that William Shakespeare and Anne Hathaway were married at Temple Grafton should be treated with very considerable scepticism, although of course it is virtually certain that the true location of their marriage will never be known.

In the case of Hillborough little has changed since Harrison's day—with no village and no proper road access it is still largely unknown and unvisited. There was a village here in the medieval period, but like many others in Warwickshire it shrank and gradually disappeared: as long ago as 1730 there were only two farms left. The dovecot, perhaps the finest in a county which is unusually rich in splendid examples of these distinctive buildings, has 900 nesting spaces. It dates from the late sixteenth century, as does the adjacent manor house. Harrison does not mention one of the greatest puzzles about Shakespeare: in November 1582 the bishop of Worcester granted him license to marry Anne Whateley of Hillborough Manor, but he did not do so, and on 26 May 1583 Susanna, his first child by Anne Hathaway, was baptised at Stratford. According to legend the second Anne was the maidservant to the first, and while courting the mistress Shakespeare fell in love with the maid. The details of the earlier betrothal, and the reasons for the sudden change, are quite obscure—although Anne Hathaway's pregnancy was presumably not without relevance.

**"Haunted" Hillborough.** —There is no village here, but only a gabled stone manor house, perhaps of early sixteenth century date, although with later alterations. It stands on the north side of the River Avon, rather more than five miles west of Stratford, and about two miles east of Bidford station. There appears to be no assignable reason for its appellation of "haunted", so that the ghost—if one ever existed—has long since been "buried". The circular stone dove-cot, close to the house, is quite an imposing building, and looks as if it were intended to stand a siege (figure 76).

Broom, like Wixford, is now close to the new line of the A46, with all the detrimental effects upon its peace and quiet which that implies. It was once a minor railway junction, but all the railways have gone—the 'disseverance of the profitable and modern from the picturesque and ancient' is less feasible with the constant noise of a busy main road.

**"Beggarly" Broom.** —Broom village stands on the River Arrow, a mile lower down the steam than Wixford. Its railway station is the "junction" of the East and West line with that of the Midland, and—as at Wixford—the station is on the west bank of the river, while the village is on the east.

76
STONE
DOVE-COT,
HILLBOROUGH.

Whether intended or not, such a disseverance of the profitable
and modern from the picturesque and ancient is highly to be
commended.

Our view (figure 77) shows the "main street" as seen from
the banks of the river. The cottages—many of them—are in
a delightful state of disrepair. Slabs of limestone serve as garden fences; thatched roofs, dilapidated house walls, patched
and rebuilt bit by bit at intervals of a century or so, combine

77 (OPPOSITE)
BROOM
VILLAGE.

The nickname 'Beggarly Broom' is here explained as referring to the decrepit
and impoverished state of the village, while other sources suggest that the
inhabitants relied on basket-making and knife-grinding rather than prosperous
farming. However, brooms were a frequent device of beggars and travellers in
English folk songs and tales, and it is possible that the name is in fact a play
on this familiar motif. Harrison is incorrect when he implies that there was
no inn: the Broom Inn is recorded as far back as the early seventeenth
century. The 'delightful state of disrepair' to which Harrison refers reminds us
that the idea of a neat, trim, tidy and well-kept country cottage, with roses
round the door and everything immaculate, is a very recent one: in the past
such cottages were decrepit, often insanitary, and always hard to maintain
and keep clean.

with the absence of an orthodox church and an inn to give a reason for the uncomplimentary title of "Beggarly Broom!"

**"Drunken" Bidford.** —Bidford is beautifully situated upon the Avon, about eight miles below Stratford, and half a mile south of Bidford station (East and West Junction Railway), which is a mere shed. It is usually visited by walking from Broom Junction (two miles). The natives seem quite proud of the title "Drunken Bidford", and firmly believe in the story of Shakespeare's potations at a substantial gabled stone house, formerly the Falcon Inn, but which, it can be proved, was *not* entitled to that distinction at the time when the "bard" could have visited it.

Bidford Church (dedicated to St. Lawrence) has an imposing look when seen from across the river. The embattled western tower and the chancel (Early English) are old, but the nave and aisles were rebuilt in 1835. Inside there are monuments to Dorothy Skipworth (died 1655) and Woodchurch Clark (1647); and the church

Bidford was off the beaten track until the motor age—Harrison's pungent description of its station as 'a mere shed' half a mile away sums up perfectly the notoriously down-at-heel finances of the East and West Junction Railway. The Falcon Inn is described by Alexandra Wedgwood as 'a stately though irregular stone house'. It stands at the end of what was once the market place of the failed medieval market town, close to the site of a market cross which in 1639 was described as 'all downe and ruinated'. When Harrison was exploring and photographing the district the inn had also fallen on hard times: in 1861 part had been turned into the Bidford Institute and Working Men's Reading Room, and the remainder had been divided into no fewer than seven tenements for labourers.

The church was drastically 'improved' during the nineteenth century. The bridge, in contrast, is largely medieval: its narrowness caused considerable difficulties once the motor car became ubiquitous. Bidford, having been a rather out-of-the-way village, found itself on the main trunk road from Coventry and Warwick through Stratford to Worcester, and it was shaken and wracked by heavy traffic. Eventually, in the 1970s, a short 'relief road' was built, to take through traffic out of the main street, but in the longer-term the building of the new routes for the A46 from Stratford, via the old A422, and then to Alcester and south to Evesham, may be of greater benefit—though the tranquil rural lifestyle which Harrison observed will never return.

THE OLD FALCON INN, BIDFORD.

78
THE FALCON
INN, BIDFORD.

plate and chest are good. Bidford was the point at which travellers by the old Roman road—the Ryknield Street—forded the Avon. But in 1482 the good monks of Alcester built a capital stone bridge a hundred yards or so below the ford, and this bridge is now the natural rendezvous of idlers and holiday makers. A stone in the parapet of the bridge, near the inn window, has served for four centuries as a hone for knives, and in its vicinity of a summer evening quite a row of men and boys may be seen "waiting their turn". A good deal of boating is done from Bidford, the favourite course being down the stream to the mill weir at Salford Priors and back.

## CHAPTER XIII

# The Warwickshire Avon—
# from source to Severn

".  .  .  Shakespeare's warblings wild:
Whom on the winding Avon's willowed banks
Fair Fancy found .  .  ."

—*Joseph Warton*, 1749.

HOSE who wish to make some real acquaintance with Shakespeare's country cannot do better than follow the course of his own river—he, the "Swan of Avon"—from its source, near Naseby, in Northamptonshire, to the point where it unites with the Severn at Tewkesbury, in Gloucestershire, a total distance of about one hundred miles. But to form this acquaintanceship the student must *walk*. We believe that only by walking over the ground can a real knowledge of any tract of country be obtained.

Many writers have discoursed about the beauties of the Warwickshire Avon. As far back as 1795 Samuel Ireland published his *Picturesque Views on the Avon*, and we also have J. Thorne's *Rambles by Rivers: The Avon*, 1845, and Mr. C. Showell's *Shakespeare's Avon*, 1901, besides countless magazine articles. But the most interesting account of the river is that contained in Mr. Quiller-Couch's *The Warwickshire Avon*, illustrated by A. Parsons, 1892, in which the author and the artist describe how they made a trip by canoe (more or less) along the entire course of the stream.

> C. Showell's *Shakespeare's Avon* of 1901 was reprinted and privately published in facsimile form in 1984, by the grandson of the author. Originals and reprints are, like the other books which Harrison lists—and like his own works—now collectors' items.

**From Naseby to Stratford.** —Rising near the battlefield of Naseby, the Avon enters what we have called "Shakespeare-Land" at Rugby. A dozen miles (as the crow flies) lower down the stream a special halt should be made to study Lord Leigh's beautiful deer park with the abbey ruins at Stoneleigh. Under one of the great oaks here tradition sets Shakespeare musing, and, indeed, the resemblance of the scene to the "Forest of Arden", in *As You Like It*, is sufficiently close. If we try to keep to the riverbank, we find that every mile in a straight line is made into two, or even three, by the windings of the steam; but Guy's Cliffe and Warwick (see p. 83) are soon left behind, and three miles below Warwick we stand on the good stone bridge at Barford. Here the walk along the cast bank of the river, through Wasperton village with its dove-cot to Charlecote and Hampton Lucy, is, indeed, such an experience as we believe no other country than England could give; and if we can trudge another four miles we may put up for the night at Stratford, rejoicing in the thought that we have spent a day with Shakespeare's own river, and with his birds and flowers, and the people of his own countryside.

> The grounds at Stoneleigh are now the permanent showground of the National Agricultural Centre, and the national show held there each year is one of the key events in the farming calendar. However, most of the deer park survives.

> Standing on the good stone bridge at Barford is not as peaceful an experience as it was in Harrison's time, because the A429 carries heavy traffic south from Warwick and the M40 into the Cotswolds. The building of the M40, with its huge interchange at Longbridge, has had a dramatic impact upon the landscape of this section of the Avon.

**From Stratford to Evesham.** —Beyond Stratford we pass familiar spots at Luddington, Welford, Hillborough, and Bidford, until, some eight miles below Bidford, we halt at the romantic spot where a ferry crosses the Avon at the Fish and Anchor Inn. From this point it is a short walk to a delightful Worcestershire village—Harvington,—where the church has

79
COTTAGES AT
HARVINGTON.

a Norman tower with a modern spire. The oak seats in the
nave bear the date 1582, so that we may pleasantly rest in
the thought that more than one Stratford man—including,
perhaps, the greatest of them all—may have strolled in just
as we have done. The thatched "black and white" cottages
of this district are very pleasant to the eye, and in some cases
the freely growing box tree is still kept clipped into the formal
shapes which delighted our ancestors.

On the opposite bank to Harvington, and a mile or so
lower down the steam, is another old-time village—Offenham,—where again thatched cottages line the rustic streets,
and open-eyed children gaze with earnestness at every
stranger.

There is no longer a ferry near Harvington, but the village itself is still
delightful, and surrounded by many acres of orchard. It is very doubtful if the
average Stratford man of the 1580s would have wandered casually into a
country church ten miles away from home—he would more likely have
regarded this part of Worcestershire as *terra incognita*!

80
OLD HOUSES
AT OFFENHAM.

**The Garden of England.** —And now we enter on one of the few spots to which the term "Garden of England" has been justly applied:

> "Great Evesham's fertile glebe what tongue hath not extolled?
> As though to her alone belonged the garb of gold."
> —Drayton.

Evesham stands just twelve miles south-west of Stratford-upon-Avon, and the connection between the two towns—especially in the palmy days of the wool trade in the sixteenth century—has always been close. The Avon encircles the town on all sides except the north, and this fact helped to complete the destruction here, in 1265, of the little army under Simon de Montfort; for his foes, in far superior numbers, under Prince Edward, came down upon him from the north, and escape in other directions was barred by the Avon. "Let us commend our souls to God," the old warrior said, "for our bodies are the foe's". De Montfort was slain at the point now called Battle Well, and in after years his corse—laid to rest under the high altar of the abbey—was reputed to work miracles.

The good bridge at Evesham is of modern construction, but Bridge Street leads us up to the market place, where the quaint old market hall stands out conspicuously. Passing

143

through a low Norman gateway, we find ourselves in front of the grand Bell tower (figure 81), built by Abbot Lichfield in 1533, and one hundred an ten feet in height—a splendid example of the Perpendicular style. The other remains of the abbey include an arch (Decorated), with the almonry, some walls, &c. Notice the two churches of St. Lawrence and of All Saints standing within the abbey churchyard, and erected by the monks for the use of the parishioners. Tradition credits the founding of Evesham Abbey to Bishop Ecgwin, in A.D. 700. But the great fabric which once stood resplendent here had the Norman gateway as part of its first erection in 1122; while the Bell tower could barely have been completed (1539) when the Dissolution came. The monks were turned adrift, and the noble abbey became a mere quarry for every builder in the district who wanted ready dressed stone; so that less than a century saw its destruction.

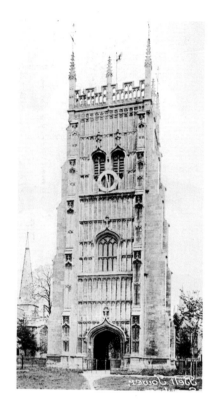

81
THE
BELL-TOWER,
EVESHAM.

Just twenty-one years after Shakespeare's death, that is to say, in 1637, one William Sandys of Fladbury expended a large sum (£20,000, it is said) in constructing locks and weirs, so that the Avon was made navigable from Tewkesbury to Stratford; and pictures of Stratford in the eighteenth and early part of the nineteenth centuries show barges sailing upon the river there. But the advent of railways ruined the waterways, and although the Avon is still more or less navigable to a point 5 miles above Evesham, yet from thence to Stratford all Mr Sandys' money has been spent in vain, for the locks and other contrivances appertaining to the maintenance of a proper depth of the water have been suffered to fall into a state of ruin and decay.

The Avon Navigation, which eventually linked with the Stratford-upon-Avon Canal running north to Birmingham, was an important commercial artery until the middle years of the nineteenth century. Then, as Harrison notes, the railways killed off its trade, and in 1875 the waterway was abandoned. Above Evesham the navigation fell into complete decay, and below that point the river was navigable for only the smallest boats. During the 1950s and early 1960s the heroic efforts of the volunteers from the Avon Navigation Trust ensured that the waterway was reopened to Evesham in 1964, and the work was subsequently extended to Stratford to link with the restored canal and so give the possibility of a superb circular route.

**From Evesham to Tewkesbury.** —The stretch of the Avon from Evesham to Tewkesbury, where it ends its course by pouring its waters into the Severn, is, if possible, still more beautiful than the upper courses of the river. For one thing, the stream is much broader and deeper, so that the boating is better, while the river-side vegetation—the reeds and rushes and flowering plants, with a background of trees—becomes something to dream about. Here are Cropthorne (maintained by good judges to be "the most beautiful village in England"), Pershore with its abbey-tower and choir and bridge, Eckington bridge, Strensham, and Twyning Ferry; while ever the great curve of Bredon Hill rises, now before, now at our side, and now behind us, as the stream winds in mystifying curves.

Lastly, the great tower of Tewkesbury Abbey comes into view, standing "four-square to all the winds that blow", and the oarsman leaves his craft at the last of the fine old stone bridges—the Mythe Bridge—which cross the Avon. A little below the bridge the discerning eye may recognize the walled garden (belonging to the Bell and Bowling-Green Inn) overlooking the stream, and the water-meadows which Mrs Craik describes so beautifully in *John Halifax, Gentleman*; while the Bell Hotel (opposite the abbey gate) is her "Phineas Fletcher's house". Mills line the river here, and the many old houses in the streets are not to be surpassed in their quaintness and good state of preservation; but every other attraction must

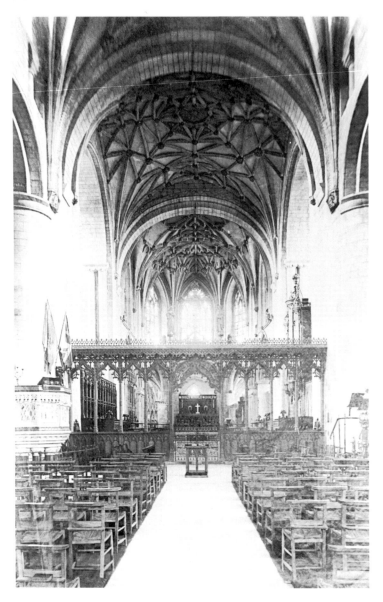

82
TEWKESBURY
ABBEY, THE
NAVE,
LOOKING EAST.

yield to the abbey. The grand arch of the west front prepares us for the noble nave, with its immense round Norman pillars, dating back to 1105 (figure 82). After the defeat of the Lancastrians by the Yorkists at the disastrous Battle of Tewkesbury, in 1471, the Duke of Somerset, with about a dozen other nobles and knights, sought sanctuary in the abbey; and when Edward IV tried to force his way to them, a brave priest, with the Host in his hand, stood at the door, and refused entrance to the king until he had promised to spare the lives of the fugitives. The promise was given, but—alas, for the royal word!—three days afterwards the duke and his companions were dragged out by a band of armed men and beheaded.

### Farewell to the Avon—and to Shakespeare-Land.

—And so at Tewkesbury we say good-bye to the Avon, and end, too, our wanderings in Shakespeare-Land. It is emphatically a district to be studied thoroughly and slowly—a land of rest. No wonder that William Shakespeare hastened to retreat to its harmonies of wood and water as soon as he was able to free himself from the demands of the stage and the metropolis.

Every year more and more students flock to the poet's shrine, and we would urge them not to be content—as so many are—with a hurried stay at Stratford-upon-Avon, but to visit and dwell upon the many other spots connected with his history and that of his family, of which we have tried to give some description in this brief account of Shakespeare-Land.